Breakfast & Brunch

100+ RECIPES TO START THE DAY

weldon**owen**

CONTENTS

INTRODUCTION

From crisp waffles with buttery-sweet dulce de leche, fried eggs with asparagus and pancetta, and cacio e pepe mini scones to golden hash browns, this book covers the full spectrum of choices for the first meal of the day.

Breakfast or brunch provides fuel and flavor for both your body and mind, and the decision of what to eat is driven by an ever-changing combination of factors: nutrition, favorite seasonal ingredients, and nostalgia. And the choices we make each morning go a long way toward setting the tone for the day ahead.

Breakfast can be a quick grab-and-go meal while rushing out the door to work—think Overnight Oats with Cocoa Nibs & Raspberry Compote (page 99)—or enjoyed leisurely on slow-paced mornings, when you can relax and savor your meal over a strong cup of coffee and unhurried conversation. Brunch can be a festive occasion with friends served alfresco, or a merry holiday gathering where multiple dishes are served family style.

This book shows you how to make the classics—eggs and bacon, pancakes, French toast, and muffins—along with plenty of variations for personalizing them. It also embraces flavors from around the world with dishes like flavor-packed North African shakshuka (page 30), Middle Eastern Za'atar Fried Eggs with Herb Salad & Yogurt (page 26), Mexican-inspired Huevos Rancheros (page 20), and Fried Egg, Bacon & Cheddar Sandwiches with Chile Crunch Mayo (page 10).

Easier access to a world pantry of ingredients and a better understanding of nutrition have also influenced morning meals. Breakfasts that star healthful grains, nuts, and seeds along with fresh fruit, fiber-rich oatmeal, protein-packed eggs, and whole-grain toast create nourishing fare. Try Chia Pudding with Fruit Compote (page 105), Soft-Boiled Eggs with Aleppo Chile Salt (page 34), Steel-Cut Oats with Honey-Glazed Pears & Pecans (page 101), and Kabocha Squash Toasts with Goat Cheese & Pepitas (page 125).

Breakfast & Brunch celebrates the morning meal as a time to renew and replenish with delicious food and good company. The inspiring recipes here give breakfast cooks plenty of ideas and flexibility, from the most scrumptious versions of beloved dishes to creative, innovative flavor combinations that nourish and satisfy.

EGGS

Fried Egg, Bacon & Cheddar Sandwiches with Chile Crunch Mayo 10

Fried Eggs with Asparagus, Pancetta & Bread Crumbs 13

Mushroom, Spinach & Feta Omelet 14

Cajun Sausage, Bell Pepper, Green Onion & Jack Scramble 16

Potato, Egg & Cheese Breakfast Tacos 17

Flank Steak Hash with Poached Eggs 19

Huevos Rancheros 20

Tex-Mex Migas 22

Polenta with Poached Eggs, Prosciutto & Pecorino 23

Caprese Scramble with Cherry Tomatoes, Basil & Mozzarella 25

Za'atar Fried Eggs with Herb Salad & Yogurt 26

Smoked Salmon, Crème Fraîche & Chive Scramble 27

Eggs Blackstone with Roasted Tomatoes 28

Shakshuka with Feta & Farro 30

Roasted Red Pepper, Potato & Herb Frittata 31

Ham, Leek & Gruyère Quiche 33

Soft-Boiled Eggs with Aleppo Chile Salt 34

Deviled Eggs with Lemon Zest, Chives & Capers 35

Basic Eggs 36

FRIED EGG, BACON & CHEDDAR SANDWICHES WITH CHILE CRUNCH MAYO

MAKES 4 SERVINGS

½ cup (120 ml) mayonnaise

2–4 tbsp chile crunch

8 large slices thick-cut applewood-smoked bacon

6 tbsp (90 g) unsalted butter, at room temperature

4 large eggs

Kosher salt and freshly ground pepper

8 slices rustic country bread

½ lb (225 g) sharp Cheddar cheese, thinly sliced

8 thick slices ripe tomato, drained on paper towels

A great breakfast sandwich relies on the sum of its parts: fresh eggs, crisp bacon, slices of ripe tomato, and melty cheese all on your favorite rustic bread. Add a swipe of umami-rich chile crunch mayo to really take it over the top. If you like, swap out the bacon for ham or a sausage patty or omit the meat for a veggie version.

In a small bowl, stir together the mayonnaise and 2 tbsp of the chile crunch. Taste and add more chile crunch if you like. Set aside.

In a large frying pan, cook the bacon over medium heat, turning a few times, until crisp and brown, about 8 minutes. Transfer to paper towels to drain. Discard the fat in the pan. Rinse the pan with water and wipe clean with paper towels. Cut each bacon slice in half crosswise and set aside.

In the same pan, melt 2 tbsp of the butter over medium heat. Crack the eggs into the pan. Season with salt and pepper, cover, reduce the heat to medium-low, and cook until the whites are set and the yolks thicken, 2–3 minutes for sunny-side up eggs. Or carefully flip the eggs and cook to the desired doneness.

Lay 4 of the bread slices on a work surface and spread each with 1 tbsp chile crunch mayo, then top each with a slice of the cheese, 2 tomato slices, one-fourth of the bacon, 1 egg, and the remaining cheese. Spread the remaining bread slices with 1 tbsp of chile crunch mayo, then top each sandwich with a bread slice, mayo side down.

Spread the outsides of each sandwich with 1 tbsp of the remaining butter. Return the frying pan to medium heat or preheat an electric panini press according to the manufacturer's directions. Add the sandwiches. Place a flat lid or a heatproof plate on top of the sandwiches in the frying pan to weight them down, or cover the press.

Cook until golden brown, about 4 minutes total. (If using a frying pan, turn the sandwiches to cook both sides, weighting the other side down to compress the sandwiches.)

Cut the sandwiches in half and serve.

FRIED EGGS WITH ASPARAGUS, PANCETTA & BREAD CRUMBS

MAKES 4 SERVINGS

16 medium-thick asparagus spears, tough ends removed

Olive oil for drizzling

Kosher salt and freshly ground pepper

2 tsp plus 2 tbsp unsalted butter

2 thin slices pancetta, chopped

½ cup (20 g) fresh coarse bread crumbs

¼ tsp minced fresh thyme or rosemary

4 large eggs

Grated Parmesan cheese for garnish (optional)

This dish is elegant enough for the most festive of brunches but is so easy to put together, you can serve it for a weeknight breakfast for dinner. Roasted asparagus and fried eggs are topped with crispy pancetta and herb-flecked bread crumbs for a meal not to be missed.

Preheat the oven to 400°F (200°C).

Spread the asparagus in a baking dish large enough to hold the spears in a single layer. Drizzle with the oil and season with salt and pepper. Toss to coat evenly. Roast the asparagus, turning once or twice, until tender-crisp, about 15 minutes; the timing will depend on the thickness of the spears. Remove from the oven and loosely cover with aluminum foil.

In a small frying pan, melt the 2 tsp butter over medium-high heat. Add the pancetta and cook, stirring occasionally, until it just darkens slightly, about 1 minute. Add the bread crumbs and thyme and cook, stirring occasionally, until golden, about 2 minutes. Remove from the heat.

In a large frying pan, melt the remaining 2 tbsp butter over medium-high heat. Break the eggs into the pan, spacing them about 1 inch (2.5 cm) apart. Reduce the heat to low and season the eggs with salt and pepper. Cover and cook until the whites are set and the yolks begin to firm around the edges, 5–7 minutes.

Just before the eggs are ready, arrange the asparagus on plates. Transfer the eggs to the plates. Sprinkle the eggs and asparagus with the bread crumb mixture. Garnish with cheese (if using) and serve.

MUSHROOM, SPINACH & FETA OMELET

MAKES 2 OMELETS

2 tbsp unsalted butter

¼ lb (115 g) cremini mushrooms, sliced

3 oz (90 g) baby spinach

½ tsp minced fresh oregano

¼ tsp kosher salt, plus more as needed

Freshly ground pepper

4 large eggs

2 tbsp whole milk

½ cup (70 g) crumbled feta cheese

With a little practice and a good-quality nonstick pan, making omelets can become a morning ritual. Start simply with a good melting cheese and maybe some chopped fresh herbs. This Greek-style omelet with mushrooms, spinach, and feta is a favorite. To change it up, add chopped, crisp-cooked bacon or swap out the feta for shredded Cheddar or crumbled goat cheese. Serve with sausage and Roasted Rosemary Potatoes (page 152).

In a frying pan, preferably nonstick, melt 1 tbsp of the butter over medium heat. Add the mushrooms and cook, stirring occasionally, until the juices evaporate and the mushrooms begin to brown, about 6 minutes. Stir in the spinach and cook, stirring, until wilted, about 1 minute. (If there is any excess water, drain it off). Stir in the oregano and season with salt and pepper. Transfer to a bowl and set aside.

Preheat the oven to 200°F (95°C).

In a bowl, whisk together the eggs, milk, ¼ tsp salt, and a few grinds of pepper just until blended.

In the same frying pan, melt ½ tbsp of the butter over medium heat until hot. Tilt the pan to cover the bottom evenly with butter.

Add half of the egg mixture to the pan and cook until the eggs have barely begun to set around the edges, about 30 seconds. Using a heatproof spatula, lift the cooked edges and gently push them toward the center, tilting the pan to allow the liquid egg on top to flow underneath, then cook for 30 seconds. Repeat this process two more times. When the eggs are almost completely set but still slightly moist on top, sprinkle half of the cheese over half of the omelet. Scatter half of the mushroom-spinach mixture over the cheese.

Using the spatula, fold the untopped half of the omelet over the filled half to create a half-moon shape. Cook the omelet for 30 seconds longer, then slide it onto a heatproof serving plate. Keep warm in the oven. Repeat to make a second omelet in the same manner. Serve at once.

CAJUN SAUSAGE, BELL PEPPER & JACK SCRAMBLE

MAKES 4-6 SERVINGS

2 tsp olive oil

½ lb (225 g) andouille or other spicy smoked sausage, cubed

½ cup (70 g) chopped green bell pepper

½ cup (70 g) chopped red bell pepper

2 green onions, white and green parts, minced

1 clove garlic, minced

12 large eggs

½ tsp kosher salt

¼ tsp hot pepper sauce

2 tbsp unsalted butter

½ cup (60 g) shredded Monterey Jack or Cheddar cheese

Scrambling is a quick and almost foolproof way to cook eggs and is also delightfully versatile. Add a sprinkle of cheese and some veggies or meat and you have an endless combination of flavors. This Cajun version features smoked andouille sausage, green and red bell peppers, green onions, and a splash of hot pepper sauce.

In a large frying pan, warm the oil over medium-high heat. Add the sausage and cook, stirring occasionally, until it begins to brown, about 5 minutes. Add the bell peppers, reduce the heat to medium, cover, and cook, stirring occasionally, until the peppers are tender, about 4 minutes. Uncover and add the green onions and garlic. Cook, stirring occasionally, until the garlic softens and is fragrant, about 2 minutes. Transfer the sausage mixture to a medium bowl and cover with aluminum foil to keep warm.

In a large bowl, whisk together the eggs, salt, and hot pepper sauce until just thoroughly blended. Do not overbeat.

In the same frying pan, melt the butter over medium-low heat. Add the egg mixture to the pan and cook until the eggs begin to set, about 20 seconds. Stir with a heatproof spatula, scraping up the eggs on the bottom and sides of the pan and folding them toward the center. Repeat until the eggs are barely cooked into moist curds.

Add the sausage mixture and the cheese and stir to distribute throughout the eggs. Remove the pan from the heat and let the eggs stand in the pan to allow the residual heat to finish cooking them and melt the cheese, about 1 minute. Serve at once.

POTATO, EGG & CHEESE BREAKFAST TACOS

MAKES 4 SERVINGS

2 russet potatoes, scrubbed

¾ tsp kosher salt, plus more as needed

2 tbsp olive oil

1 small yellow onion, finely chopped

¼ tsp freshly ground pepper, plus more as needed

8 large eggs

1 tbsp unsalted butter

8 flour tortillas, each about 6 inches (15 cm) in diameter, warmed

1 cup (115 g) shredded Monterey Jack or Cheddar cheese

Pico de Gallo (page 157) or your favorite salsa for serving

There are countless variations on what you can include with fluffy scrambled eggs tucked into warm tortillas. Pan-fried potatoes and shredded cheese are a terrific starting point for a hearty breakfast taco. Swap out the flour tortillas for corn tortillas if you prefer, and have fun adding other veggies or meats to create your ultimate breakfast dish.

Put the potatoes in a large saucepan and add enough cold salted water to cover. Bring to a boil over high heat. Reduce the heat to medium-low and simmer until the potatoes are tender when pierced with the tip of a knife, about 25 minutes. Drain and rinse under cold running water. Refrigerate until chilled, at least 2 hours or up to overnight.

Peel the potatoes and cut into small cubes. In a large frying pan, preferably nonstick, warm the oil over medium-high heat. Add the potato cubes and cook, stirring occasionally, until browned, about 10 minutes. Add the onion and cook, stirring often, until softened, about 4 minutes. Remove from the heat and season with salt and pepper.

Meanwhile, in a bowl, whisk together the eggs, ¾ tsp salt, and ¼ tsp pepper just until thoroughly blended. Return the pan with the potatoes to medium-low heat. Add the egg mixture to the pan and cook until the eggs begin to set, about 20 seconds. Stir with a heatproof spatula, scraping up the eggs on the bottom and sides of the pan and folding them toward the center. Repeat until the eggs are barely cooked into moist curds. Remove the pan from the heat and let stand to allow the residual heat to finish cooking the eggs, about 1 minute.

Fill the tortillas with equal amounts of the potato-egg mixture, sprinkle with the cheese, and top with a spoonful of pico de gallo. Serve at once.

VARIATION
Add crisp-cooked bacon, diced ham, or cooked and crumbled Mexican-style chorizo to the potato-egg mixture.

FLANK STEAK HASH WITH POACHED EGGS

MAKES 4–6 SERVINGS

Unsalted butter for greasing

2 tbsp olive oil

1 yellow onion, chopped

1 red bell pepper, seeded
and chopped

1 yellow bell pepper, seeded
and chopped

1 small green bell pepper, seeded
and chopped

1 tsp ground cumin

3 Yukon gold potatoes, about
1 lb (450 g) total, cut into
½-inch (12-mm) dice

1 lb (450 g) flank steak, cut into
½-inch (12-mm) dice

2 tomatoes, peeled, seeded,
and chopped

2 tbsp heavy cream

Kosher salt and freshly ground pepper

1½ cups (170 g) panko bread crumbs

½ cup (115 g) unsalted butter, melted

4–6 Poached Eggs (page 37)

"Hash" can describe any number of meat-and-potato preparations, or even root veggie combos, all cooked up in a large frying pan for a medley of textures and flavors. This version uses diced flank steak, a colorful mix of bell peppers, potatoes, and a toasty panko bread crumb topping that gives the finished dish a wonderfully crunchy texture. A runny poached egg ties everything together.

Preheat the oven to 375°F (190°C). Grease a 2-qt (1.9-l) baking dish with butter.

In a large frying pan, warm the oil over medium-high heat. Add the onion, bell peppers, and cumin and cook, stirring frequently, until the vegetables are softened, 5–7 minutes. Add the potatoes, reduce the heat to medium, cover, and cook, stirring often, until they are almost tender but still hold their shape, about 15 minutes. When you stir, be sure to scrape the bottom of the pan to ensure the potatoes don't stick. Add 1 tbsp water if the pan becomes too dry.

Stir in the steak and tomatoes, raise the heat to medium-high, and cook, stirring frequently, until the meat shows no traces of pink, 3–5 minutes. Stir in the cream and season with salt and pepper. Transfer to the prepared baking dish. (At this point, the hash can be covered tightly and refrigerated for up to 1 day before baking.)

Sprinkle the panko over the hash and drizzle with the melted butter. Bake until the top is golden brown and the hash is heated through, about 15 minutes (or a little longer if the dish has been refrigerated).

Serve at once, topping each serving with a poached egg.

HUEVOS RANCHEROS

MAKES 4 SERVINGS

FOR THE RANCHERO SAUCE

1 tbsp avocado oil or canola oil

1 small yellow onion, chopped

½ jalapeño chile, seeded and minced

2 cloves garlic, minced

1 can (410 g) diced tomatoes
with juices

½ cup (120 ml) canned tomato sauce

1 tsp chili powder

1 canned chipotle pepper in adobo,
chopped, plus 1 tsp adobo sauce
(optional)

Kosher salt and freshly ground pepper

¼ cup (60 ml) avocado oil or canola oil

8 corn tortillas, each 6 inches (15 cm)
in diameter

8 large eggs

Kosher salt and freshly ground pepper

½ cup (70 g) crumbled queso fresco
or feta cheese

Chopped fresh cilantro for serving

Cooked black beans, warmed,
for serving

This popular breakfast dish—a hearty combination of fried corn tortillas topped with eggs, crumbled fresh cheese, and spicy ranchero sauce—originated in rural Mexico. If you like, add sliced avocado and a dollop of Mexican crema. For brunch, offer guests an icy cold Watermelon-Lime Aqua Fresca (page 134).

To make the ranchero sauce, in a saucepan, warm the oil over medium heat. Add the onion, chile, and garlic and cook, stirring occasionally, until softened, about 5 minutes. Transfer to a blender.

Add the tomatoes and their juices, tomato sauce, chili powder, and chipotle pepper and sauce (if using) to the blender and puree until smooth. Return to the saucepan and bring to a boil over high heat. Reduce the heat to medium-low and cook, stirring frequently, until reduced to about 2 cups (475 ml), about 30 minutes. Season with salt and pepper. Cover and keep warm over very low heat.

Preheat the oven to 200°F (95°C). Have ready 4 ovenproof plates large enough to hold 2 overlapping tortillas.

In a large frying pan, warm 2 tbsp of the oil over high heat. One at a time, fry the tortillas just until they begin to crisp (they should not be crunchy), about 30 seconds. Transfer to paper towels to drain. Overlap 2 tortillas on each plate and keep warm in the oven. Discard the oil in the pan.

In the same frying pan, warm the remaining 2 tbsp oil over medium heat. Crack 4 of the eggs into the pan. Season with salt and pepper, cover, reduce the heat to medium-low, and cook until the whites are set, about 2 minutes for sunny-side up eggs. Or carefully flip the eggs and cook to the desired doneness.

Transfer 2 eggs to each of 2 plates in the oven, placing them on the tortillas, and keep warm while frying the remaining eggs.

For each serving, spoon about ½ cup (120 ml) of the warm ranchero sauce over and around the eggs, top with one-fourth of the cheese, and sprinkle with cilantro. Serve hot. Pass the beans at the table.

TEX-MEX MIGAS

10 large eggs

½ tsp kosher salt

¼ tsp freshly ground pepper

2 tbsp avocado oil or canola oil

2 cups (475 ml) Pico de Gallo (page 157) or store-bought

1½ cups (130 g) coarsely broken thick tortilla chips

½ cup (60 g) shredded sharp Cheddar cheese

½ cup (60 g) shredded Monterey Jack cheese

1 cup (240 ml) Ranchero Sauce (page 20), warmed

A much-loved Tex-Mex breakfast, migas are a delicious blend of scrambled eggs, pico de gallo, crisp tortilla chips, and melty cheese. Serve them with your favorite salsa, such as the Ranchero Sauce (page 20), and warm flour or corn tortillas.

In a large bowl, whisk together the eggs, salt, and pepper.

In a large frying pan, preferably nonstick, warm the oil over medium-high heat. Add half of the pico de gallo and cook until the onion softens, about 1 minute. Add the egg mixture to the pan and cook until the eggs begin to set, about 20 seconds. Stir with a heatproof spatula, scraping up the eggs on the bottom and sides of the pan and folding them toward the center. Repeat until the eggs are just beginning to form moist curds, about 1 minute.

Add the tortilla chips and stir to distribute throughout the eggs. Cook, stirring occasionally, until the eggs are barely cooked into moist curds, about 1 minute longer. Remove the pan from the heat and let the eggs stand in the pan to allow the residual heat to finish cooking them, about 1 minute.

In a bowl, combine the cheeses. Divide the migas among 4 plates. Top each serving with a few tablespoons of the ranchero sauce and sprinkle with ¼ cup (30 g) of the cheese mixture. Serve at once and pass the remaining ranchero sauce and pico de gallo on the side.

POLENTA WITH POACHED EGGS, PROSCIUTTO & PECORINO

MAKES 4 SERVINGS

2 tsp olive oil

8 thin slices prosciutto

3 cups (700 ml) water, plus more as needed

1½ tsp kosher salt, plus more as needed

1 cup (155 g) coarse-ground polenta

1 cup (240 ml) whole milk

2 tbsp distilled white vinegar

4 large eggs

½ cup (60 g) grated pecorino cheese

Freshly ground pepper

Creamy polenta topped with poached eggs, crisp-cooked prosciutto, and nutty pecorino cheese might be the most comforting breakfast imaginable. For the best flavor, use coarsely ground polenta—not instant. If you like, stir more pecorino and some chopped fresh spinach into the polenta at the end of cooking.

In a large frying pan, warm the oil over medium heat. Add the prosciutto slices in a single layer and cook, turning once, until the slices are hot and begin to crisp at the edges, about 5 minutes. Remove from the heat and keep warm.

To make the polenta, in a large, heavy saucepan, bring the water and salt to a boil over medium-high heat. In a small bowl, stir together the polenta and milk. Gradually stir the polenta mixture into the boiling water. Stirring constantly, bring the mixture to a boil. Reduce the heat to medium-low and cook, stirring frequently, until the polenta is thick and creamy, about 25 minutes. Add up to ½ cup (120 ml) water, 1 tbsp at a time, if the polenta begins to stick. (Be careful, as the hot polenta can bubble and splatter.)

To poach the eggs, pour water to a depth of 2 inches (5 cm) into a large, deep sauté pan and add the vinegar. Bring to a gentle simmer over medium-low heat. Fill a bowl halfway with hot tap water and place it near the stove. One at a time, crack the eggs into a ramekin or small cup and gently slide the egg into the simmering water. Adjust the heat to keep the water at a gentle simmer. Cook until the whites are set and the yolks are glazed over but still soft, 4–5 minutes. Using a slotted spoon, lift each egg from the water and slip it into the hot water.

About 1 minute before the eggs are done, spoon the polenta on plates or in shallow bowls. Lay 2 prosciutto slices over each serving. Using a slotted spoon, lift each egg from the water, draining well and blotting the bottom briefly on paper towels. Trim any ragged edges of egg white with kitchen scissors. Place on the prosciutto and sprinkle each egg with 2 tbsp of the cheese. Season lightly with salt and pepper and serve.

CAPRESE SCRAMBLE WITH CHERRY TOMATOES, BASIL & MOZZARELLA

MAKES 4–6 SERVINGS

2 tsp olive oil

1 tbsp minced shallot

1 cup (170 g) cherry or grape tomatoes, halved

¾ tsp kosher salt, plus more as needed

¼ tsp freshly ground pepper, plus more as needed

12 large eggs

2 tbsp chopped fresh basil

1 tbsp unsalted butter

¼ lb (115 g) fresh mozzarella cheese, cubed

Bring summer to your breakfast plate with this caprese salad meets scrambled eggs mash-up. Perfect for an alfresco brunch, it would be excellent paired with a simple green salad, thick slices of toast, and peach bellinis (page 138).

In a large frying pan, warm the oil over medium heat. Add the shallot and cook, stirring occasionally, until softened, about 1 minute. Add the tomatoes and cook stirring occasionally, until hot and beginning to soften, about 2 minutes. Remove from the heat and season with salt and pepper. Transfer the tomato mixture to a medium bowl and cover with aluminum foil to keep warm.

In a large bowl, whisk together the eggs, 1 tbsp of the basil, ¾ tsp salt, and ¼ tsp pepper until just thoroughly blended. Do not overbeat. In the same frying pan, melt the butter over medium-low heat. Add the egg mixture to the pan and cook until the eggs begin to set, about 20 seconds. Stir with a heatproof spatula, scraping up the eggs on the bottom and sides of the pan and folding them toward the center. Repeat until the eggs are barely cooked into moist curds.

Add the tomato mixture and the cheese and stir to distribute throughout the eggs. Remove the pan from the heat and let the eggs stand in the pan to allow the residual heat to finish cooking them and melt the cheese, about 1 minute. Sprinkle the remaining 1 tbsp basil over the scramble and serve.

ZA'ATAR FRIED EGGS WITH HERB SALAD & YOGURT

MAKES 4 SERVINGS

5 tbsp (75 ml) olive oil

1 tbsp za'atar

½ tsp sweet paprika

½ tsp red pepper flakes (optional)

Kosher salt and freshly ground pepper

1 cup (250 g) plain yogurt

1 tsp grated lemon zest

1 tbsp fresh lemon juice

½ small clove garlic, minced

⅓ cup (20 g) roughly chopped fresh dill

⅓ cup (20 g) roughly chopped fresh flat-leaf parsley

¼ cup (15 g) roughly chopped fresh mint

8 large eggs

4 pieces flatbread, such as naan, warmed, for serving

Za'atar is a savory blend of dried herbs mixed with sesame seeds, sumac, and other earthy spices. It's often used in Middle Eastern cuisine, such as this Persian-inspired breakfast with fried eggs, a jumble of fresh herbs, and lemon-garlic yogurt. Pair it with the flatbread of your choice. If you like, swap out the yogurt for labneh, a thick, tangy cheese made from strained yogurt, and add a dollop of fig jam.

In a small bowl, stir together 4 tbsp (60 ml) of the oil, za'atar, paprika, and red pepper flakes (if using). Season to taste with salt. Set aside.

In another small bowl, stir together the yogurt, lemon zest, lemon juice, and garlic. Divide the yogurt among plates, spreading it out slightly in the center of each plate. Arrange the dill, parsley, and mint on one side of the yogurt.

In a large frying pan, preferably nonstick, warm the remaining 1 tbsp oil over medium heat. One at a time, crack 4 of the eggs into the pan. Season the eggs with salt and pepper, cover, reduce the heat to medium-low, and cook until the whites are opaque and the yolks thicken, 2–3 minutes for sunny-side up eggs. For over-easy, over-medium, or over-hard eggs, cook as directed, then carefully flip the eggs and cook for about 30 seconds for eggs over easy, about 1 minute for eggs over medium, and about 1½ minutes for eggs over hard. Transfer 1 egg to each plate. Repeat to fry the remaining 4 eggs, then add to the plates.

Drizzle the eggs and yogurt with the reserved za'atar oil. Serve the flatbread alongside.

SMOKED SALMON, CRÈME FRAÎCHE & CHIVE SCRAMBLE

MAKES 4 SERVINGS

2 tbsp unsalted butter

8 large eggs beaten with 2 tbsp whole milk

Kosher salt and freshly ground pepper

¼ lb (115 g) smoked salmon, chopped

2 tbsp chopped fresh chives, plus more for garnish

½ cup (115 g) crème fraîche, at room temperature

1 tbsp grated lemon zest

The addition of smoked salmon and fresh chives to scrambled eggs takes them from simple to sublime. Topped with dollops of creamy-tangy crème fraîche and a sprinkle of lemon zest, the dish becomes holiday-worthy fare.

In a large nonstick frying pan, melt the butter over medium-low heat. Season the egg mixture with salt and pepper and pour into the pan. Cook without stirring for 1 minute. Using a rubber spatula, gently stir the eggs, allowing the uncooked eggs to run to the bottom of the pan. Cook until the eggs are mostly set, about 3 minutes, then stir in the smoked salmon and chives. Continue to gently stir until the eggs are set, about 1 minute longer.

Divide the eggs among plates. Top each with 2 tbsp of the crème fraîche, then garnish with the lemon zest and more chives. Serve at once.

EGGS BLACKSTONE WITH ROASTED TOMATOES

MAKES 4 SERVINGS

1 tbsp olive oil, plus more for cooking

4 plum tomatoes, halved lengthwise

1 tsp minced fresh thyme

½ tsp kosher salt

¼ tsp freshly ground pepper, plus more as needed

8 large slices thick-cut applewood-smoked bacon, halved crosswise

4 English muffins, split crosswise

2 tbsp distilled white vinegar

8 large eggs

About 1 cup (240 ml) Hollandaise Sauce (page 157)

In this decadent brunch favorite, layers of thyme-roasted tomatoes and thick, crunchy bacon create a base for poached eggs topped with lemony hollandaise sauce. This dish is traditionally made with English muffins, but toasted rustic bread is a great alternative.

Preheat the oven to 400°F (200°C). Lightly oil a rimmed baking sheet.

Arrange the tomatoes, cut side up, on the prepared baking sheet. Drizzle with the oil, then sprinkle with the thyme, salt, and pepper. Roast until the tomatoes have shrunk slightly and their juices are bubbling, about 30 minutes.

In a large frying pan, fry the bacon over medium heat, turning once, until crisp and browned, about 6 minutes. Transfer to paper towels to drain.

Meanwhile, preheat the broiler. Place the muffins, cut side up, on a baking sheet and toast in the broiler until lightly crisped, about 1 minute. Remove from the broiler and set aside.

Pour water to a depth of 2 inches (5 cm) into a large, deep sauté pan and add the vinegar. Bring to a gentle simmer over medium-low heat. Fill a bowl halfway with hot tap water and place it near the stove. One at a time, crack the eggs into a ramekin or small cup and gently slide the egg into the simmering water. Cook as many eggs as will fit comfortably in the pan and adjust the heat to keep the water at a gentle simmer. Cook until the whites are set and the yolks are glazed over but still soft, 4–5 minutes. Using a slotted spoon, lift each egg from the water and slip it into the hot water.

To serve, place 2 muffin halves, cut side up, on each plate. Top each half with 2 pieces of bacon and 1 roasted tomato half. One at a time, using a slotted spoon, remove the poached eggs from the water, resting the bottom of the spoon briefly on a kitchen towel to blot excess moisture, and perch an egg on each muffin half. Spoon about 3 tbsp of hollandaise sauce over each serving, then sprinkle with pepper. Serve at once, passing the remaining hollandaise on the side.

SHAKSHUKA WITH FETA & FARRO

MAKES 6 SERVINGS

2 tbsp olive oil

½ yellow onion, chopped

1 clove garlic, chopped

½ cup (90 g) drained and chopped jarred roasted red peppers

2 tsp ground cumin

1 tsp smoked paprika

Pinch red pepper flakes

Kosher salt and freshly ground pepper

1 can (800 g) diced tomatoes with juices

4 oz (115 g) feta cheese, crumbled

6 large eggs

3 cups (510 g) cooked farro, warm

2 tbsp chopped fresh flat-leaf parsley

This North African dish features eggs baked in a spicy tomato–bell pepper sauce. Here, it's topped with feta cheese and spooned over warm, nutty farro. Substantial and flavorful, this dish makes an excellent brunch centerpiece. Serve it with warmed pita bread and slices of fresh melon.

Preheat the oven to 350°F (180°C).

In a large ovenproof frying pan, warm the oil over medium-high heat. Add the onion and cook, stirring occasionally, until softened, about 6 minutes. Add the garlic and cook, stirring occasionally, for 1 minute. Stir in the roasted peppers, cumin, paprika, and red pepper flakes. Season with salt and pepper and cook, stirring occasionally, until fragrant, about 1 minute. Stir in the tomatoes and their juices and bring to a boil. Reduce the heat to low and simmer, stirring occasionally, until thickened, about 10 minutes. Stir in half the cheese, then season to taste with salt and pepper.

Using a large spoon, create 6 wells in the sauce, spacing them evenly apart. Crack an egg into each well. Sprinkle the top with the remaining cheese. Transfer the pan to the oven and bake until the egg whites are opaque, about 10 minutes.

Divide the warm farro among bowls. Top each with an egg and a generous portion of the sauce. Sprinkle with the parsley and serve.

ROASTED RED PEPPER, POTATO & HERB FRITTATA

MAKES 4–6 SERVINGS

2 small red bell peppers

10 large eggs

2 tbsp chopped fresh cilantro, plus more for garnish

1 tbsp heavy cream or whole milk

Kosher salt and freshly ground pepper

1 tbsp olive oil

1 russet potato, peeled and diced

1 small yellow onion, diced

Essentially a crustless quiche, a frittata takes well to endless variations, such as this hearty version. If you like, top the frittata with your favorite crumbled or shredded cheese, such as feta, goat cheese, fontina, or Gruyère.

Preheat the broiler. Line a baking sheet with aluminum foil.

Cut each bell pepper in half lengthwise and remove the ribs, seeds, and stems. Place the peppers, cut side down, on the prepared baking sheet. Roast, turning the peppers as needed, until blackened all over, about 10 minutes. Transfer to a heatproof bowl, cover, and let steam for 5 minutes. With wet fingers, peel away the blackened skin, then chop the peppers. Set aside.

Preheat the oven to 425°F (220°C).

In a large bowl, whisk together the eggs, cilantro, cream, and a pinch each of salt and pepper. Set aside.

In a medium ovenproof frying pan, warm the oil over medium heat. Add the potato, season with salt and pepper, and cook, stirring occasionally, until just tender, 5–6 minutes. Add the onion and a pinch of salt and continue cooking, stirring occasionally, until the potato is golden brown and the onion is soft and translucent, 4–5 minutes. Stir in the roasted peppers and season to taste.

Reduce the heat to medium-low and add the egg mixture to the pan. Cook, stirring gently, until the eggs begin to set but do not start to scramble. Cook the eggs, undisturbed, until they begin to set around the edges, 2–3 minutes. Transfer the pan to the oven and bake until the eggs are set around the edges and just firm in the center, about 5 minutes.

Garnish the frittata with more cilantro and cut into wedges. Serve hot, warm, or at room temperature.

HAM, LEEK & GRUYÈRE QUICHE

MAKES 6–8 SERVINGS

1 Single-Crust Pie Dough round for 9-inch (23-cm) pie (page 158) or store-bought pie dough

All-purpose flour for dusting

1 small leek, white and pale green part

1 tbsp unsalted butter

Kosher salt and freshly ground pepper

1 thick slice Black Forest ham, about 6 oz (170 g), diced

2 large eggs

½ cup (120 ml) whole milk

½ cup (115 g) crème fraîche or sour cream

Heaping ½ cup (60 g) shredded Gruyère cheese

Tender leeks, diced smoky ham, and nutty Gruyère cheese give this classic quiche plenty of flavor. Starting with a buttery homemade crust will yield the best results, but purchased pie pastry is a great time-saver. For a traditional quiche Lorraine, swap out the ham for chopped cooked bacon and the leeks for sautéed yellow onion.

If making homemade dough, prepare the pie dough and chill as directed. On a lightly floured work surface, roll out the dough into an 11-inch (28-cm) round about ⅛ inch (3 mm) thick.

Drape the dough over the rolling pin and ease it into a 9-inch (23-cm) tart pan with at least 1-inch (2.5-cm) sides and a removable bottom. Press the dough into the bottom and up the sides of the pan, then fold the edge over on itself and press together. Put the pan in the freezer and chill for about 15 minutes.

Preheat the oven to 400°F (200°C).

Prick the bottom of the pie shell with a fork, then line with aluminum foil. Fill with pie weights or dried beans. Bake until the crust is set but not browned, about 12 minutes. Remove the foil and weights. Prick any bubbles with a fork. Continue to bake until the crust is firm and very lightly golden, about 5 minutes. Transfer the pan to a wire rack.

Position the rack in the upper third of the oven and reduce the temperature to 375°F (190°C).

While the crust is baking, quarter the leek lengthwise and slice; you should have about 1 cup (90 g). In a frying pan, melt the butter over medium heat. Add the leek, season with salt, and cook, stirring occasionally, until the leek is lightly browned and tender, about 3 minutes. Add the ham, stir to combine with the leek, and remove from the heat.

In a bowl, whisk together the eggs, milk, crème fraîche, a pinch of salt, and a few grinds of pepper. Scatter the ham-leek mixture over the crust, pour in the egg mixture, and sprinkle the cheese on top.

Place the pan on a rimmed baking sheet. Bake until the quiche is puffed and lightly golden and a knife inserted into the center comes out clean, 25–30 minutes. If you like, slide the quiche under the broiler for a few minutes to brown the top a bit more.

Transfer the pan to a wire rack and let the quiche cool for about 10 minutes.

SOFT-BOILED EGGS WITH ALEPPO CHILE SALT

MAKES 2-4 SERVINGS

½ tsp dried rosemary leaves
1 tbsp kosher salt
1 tbsp Aleppo chile powder
4 large eggs

Preparing a perfectly soft-boiled egg seems like a simple task but the timing is critical. Gently bringing the eggs up to temperature from cold to simmering water, then letting them sit in the hot water ensures they stay tender and don't get rubbery. The rosemary-Aleppo chile salt takes these from everyday to superstar status.

In a spice grinder or a mortar with a pestle, grind the rosemary leaves until they are a fine powder. Transfer to a small bowl and add the salt and chile powder. Mix well with a fork. (The spice mixture can be stored in a jar with a tight-fitting lid for up to 1 month.)

Place the eggs in a saucepan and add cold water to cover by 1 inch (2.5 cm). Bring to a boil over medium-high heat. When the water boils, remove the pan from the heat and cover. Let stand for 4–5 minutes for a soft egg, 6–7 minutes for a medium-soft egg, or 8 minutes for a medium egg. Using a slotted spoon, remove the eggs. Pour off the hot water and fill the pan with cold water and ice. Return the eggs to the pan and let cool for 5 minutes.

Peel the eggs and halve lengthwise. Season with the chile salt and serve.

DEVILED EGGS WITH LEMON ZEST, CHIVES & CAPERS

MAKES 4–6 SERVINGS

6 large eggs

1 tbsp mayonnaise

1 tbsp Dijon mustard

2 tbsp minced fresh chives, plus more for garnish

1½ tbsp capers, rinsed, drained, patted dry, and coarsely chopped

2 tsp grated lemon zest

1 tsp minced shallots

¼ tsp kosher salt

¼ tsp freshly ground pepper

Deviled eggs might not sound like your typical breakfast or brunch dish, but put out a platter during any morning gathering and watch them disappear. This version adds tangy lemon zest, fresh chives, and briny capers for a whole new savory take on deviled eggs.

Place the eggs in a large saucepan and add cold water to cover by 1 inch (2.5 cm). Bring to a boil over medium-high heat. When the water boils, remove the pan from the heat and cover. Let stand for 20 minutes. Using a slotted spoon, remove the eggs. Pour off the hot water and fill the pan with cold water and ice. Return the eggs to the pan and let cool for 5 minutes. Remove the eggs and peel them under cold running water.

Cut the eggs in half lengthwise. Carefully remove the yolks and place in a bowl. Set the whites aside. Add the mayonnaise, mustard, chives, capers, lemon zest, shallots, salt, and pepper to the yolks. Using a fork, mash together until the yolk mixture is smooth and fluffy.

Spoon the yolk mixture into the cavity of each egg-white half, mounding it slightly. Arrange the deviled eggs on a plate and serve at once. Or, cover and refrigerate for up to 4 hours.

BASIC EGGS

Eggs are a perfect package of flavor, protein, and versatility—and are an ideal way to kick-start your day. Cooking eggs just right has as much to do with technique as with personal preference. Here, we'll show you the tried-and-true methods for frying, scrambling, and poaching eggs, which you can modify to suit your taste.

FRIED EGGS should be cooked over medium-low heat to ensure even cooking.

SCRAMBLED EGGS cook best in a well-seasoned or nonstick frying pan over gentle heat until soft and creamy.

POACHED EGGS cook easily in 2 inches of simmering water with a splash of vinegar.

Fried Eggs

2 tbsp olive oil or unsalted butter

8 large eggs

Kosher salt and freshly ground pepper

In a large frying pan, preferably nonstick, heat 1 tbsp of the oil over medium heat. One at a time, crack 4 of the eggs into the pan. Sprinkle the eggs with salt and pepper, cover, reduce the heat to medium-low, and cook until the whites are opaque and the yolks thicken, 2–3 minutes for sunny-side up eggs. Repeat with the remaining 1 tbsp oil and 4 eggs. Serve at once. To make over-easy, over-medium, or over-hard eggs, cook as directed, then, using a nonstick spatula, carefully flip the eggs and cook for about 30 seconds for eggs over easy, about 1 minute for eggs over medium, and about 1½ minutes for eggs over hard.

NOTE: Start with cold eggs directly from the refrigerator. The yolks are more likely to stay intact when you crack the eggs.

Scrambled Eggs

12 large eggs
¾ tsp kosher salt
¼ tsp freshly ground pepper
2 tbsp unsalted butter

In a bowl, whisk together the eggs, salt, and pepper until just thoroughly blended. Do not overbeat. In a large frying pan, preferably nonstick, melt the butter over medium-low heat until the foam begins to subside. Add the egg mixture to the pan and cook until the eggs just begin to set, about 20 seconds. Stir with a heatproof spatula, scraping up the eggs on the bottom and sides of the pan and folding them toward the center. Repeat until the eggs are barely cooked into moist curds, about 3 minutes. Remove the pan from the heat and let the eggs stand in the pan to allow the residual heat to finish cooking them, about 1 minute. Serve at once.

Poached Eggs

2 tbsp distilled white vinegar
8 large eggs

Pour water to a depth of 2 inches (5 cm) into a large, deep sauté pan and add the vinegar. Bring to a gentle simmer over medium-low heat. Fill a bowl halfway with hot tap water and place it near the stove. One at a time, crack the eggs into a ramekin or small cup and gently slide the egg into the simmering water. Cook as many eggs as will fit comfortably in the pan and adjust the heat to keep the water at a gentle simmer. Cook until the whites are set and the yolks are glazed over but still soft, 4–5 minutes. Using a slotted spoon, lift each egg from the water and slip it into the hot water. Just before serving, remove from the hot water with a slotted spoon, draining well and blotting the bottom of each egg briefly on paper towels. Trim any ragged edges of egg white with kitchen scissors. Serve at once.

PANCAKES, WAFFLES & MORE

Overnight Pumpkin Spice French Toast with Caramelized Pears 41

Almond-Crusted French Toast with Strawberry-Rhubarb Compote 42

Mascarpone Cream Crepes with Blackberry Jam 45

Banana Dulce de Leche Waffles 46

Fried Chicken with Cornmeal Waffles 47

Matcha-Glazed Buttermilk Doughnuts 48

Raised Glazed Doughnuts 52

Lemon-Ricotta Pancakes with Blueberry Compote 55

Nectarine Oven Pancake 56

Pancakes 59

Sweet Potato Pancakes with Pecans and Brown-Sugar Sauce 61

Savory Bacon, Cheddar & Green Onion Pancakes 62

Potato Latkes with Sour Cream & Applesauce 63

OVERNIGHT PUMPKIN SPICE FRENCH TOAST WITH CARAMELIZED PEARS

This cross between bread pudding and French toast is an ideal make-ahead brunch dish. Choose bread with a soft, thin crust, but opt for a good-quality artisan white bread from the bakery rather than a regular packaged brand. Use apples instead of pears if you like, or omit the fruit (or swap in sliced bananas) and serve the French toast drizzled with maple syrup.

MAKES 6–8 SERVINGS

FOR THE FRENCH TOAST

3 tbsp unsalted butter, at room temperature, plus more for greasing

1-lb (450-g) loaf good-quality sliced white bread, preferably day-old

6 large eggs

2 cups (475 ml) whole milk

½ cup (120 ml) heavy cream

½ cup (100 g) firmly packed light brown sugar

1½ tsp pumpkin pie spice

1 tsp pure vanilla extract

½ tsp kosher salt

FOR THE CARAMELIZED PEARS

1 tbsp unsalted butter

3 tbsp firmly packed light brown sugar

3 firm but ripe pears, such as Bosc or Anjou, cored and sliced

Juice of ½ lemon

Generously butter a 9-by-13-inch (23-by-33-cm) baking dish.

To make the French toast, spread 1 side of the bread slices with the butter. Lay the slices in the prepared dish so that they overlap slightly. In a bowl, whisk together the eggs, milk, cream, brown sugar, pumpkin pie spice, vanilla, and salt. Pour the egg mixture over the bread, gently pressing down on the bread so it absorbs the egg mixture. Cover with plastic wrap and refrigerate overnight.

Preheat the oven to 350°F (180°C). Remove the plastic wrap from the dish. If any of the egg mixture hasn't soaked into the bread, pour it off into a cup and drizzle over the bread with the egg mixture. Bake until puffed and golden brown, about 40 minutes. Let stand for about 10 minutes before serving.

Meanwhile, make the pears: In a large frying pan, melt the butter over medium-high heat. Add the brown sugar, pears, and lemon juice and cook, stirring occasionally, until the pears are tender and sticky, about 8 minutes. Cover to keep warm.

Serve the warm French toast with the caramelized pears.

ALMOND-CRUSTED FRENCH TOAST WITH STRAWBERRY-RHUBARB COMPOTE

MAKES 4 SERVINGS

FOR THE STRAWBERRY-RHUBARB COMPOTE

4 cups (680 g) coarsely chopped rhubarb

1½ cups (210 g) strawberries, hulled and halved

¼ cup (50 g) sugar

¼ cup (60 ml) water

6 large eggs

1 cup (240 ml) half-and-half

2 tbsp sugar

Grated zest of 1 orange

½ tsp pure vanilla extract

8 thick slices challah or brioche bread, preferably day-old

Avocado oil or canola oil for cooking

1 cup (90 g) sliced almonds

French toast is a great way to use up day-old bread—the drier the slices, the more they will absorb the egg mixture. Egg-enriched doughs such as challah or brioche produce a richly decadent dish, but you can swap in any soft-crusted country-style white bread. This is also delicious served with Blueberry Compote (page 55) or fresh mixed berries.

To make the compote, in a saucepan, combine the rhubarb, strawberries, sugar, and water. Place over medium heat and bring to a boil, then reduce the heat to medium-low and simmer until the fruit releases its juices and becomes tender, about 10 minutes. Remove from the heat and cover to keep warm. (The compote can be made up to 3 days in advance and stored in an airtight container in the refrigerator; warm over low heat before serving.)

Preheat the oven to 350°F (180°C). In a large, shallow bowl, whisk together the eggs, half-and-half, sugar, orange zest, and vanilla. Add the bread slices and turn gently to coat evenly. Let stand until the bread has soaked up some of the egg mixture, about 1 minute.

Heat a griddle or large frying pan over medium heat until hot. Lightly oil the griddle and a baking sheets. Spread the almonds on a plate. One slice at a time, remove the bread from the egg mixture, letting the excess liquid drip back into the bowl. Dip one side of the bread into the almonds, pressing gently to help the nuts adhere. Place on an ungreased baking sheet.

Working in batches if needed, the bread slices on the griddle, almond side down, and cook until the nuts begin to brown, about 2 minutes. Turn and cook until golden brown on the second sides, about 2 minutes. Transfer to the greased baking sheet, almond side down, and bake until the center of the bread is heated through but still moist, about 10 minutes.

Serve the French toast topped with the warm compote.

MASCARPONE CREAM CREPES WITH BLACKBERRY JAM

For the best crepes, be sure to mix the ingredients completely so there are no lumps remaining (a blender works best for this), then let the batter rest for at least a couple of hours. Use any kind of jam you like, such as raspberry or strawberry. Or toss fresh blackberries, raspberries, or sliced strawberries with a little granulated sugar and let stand until juicy, then serve alongside the crepes.

MAKES 4–6 SERVINGS

FOR THE CREPES

1 cup (240 ml) whole milk

2 large eggs

¼ cup (60 ml) water

3 tbsp unsalted butter, melted, plus more for cooking

1 cup (115 g) all-purpose flour

2 tbsp sugar

¼ tsp kosher salt

FOR THE MASCARPONE CREAM FILLING

1 cup (240 ml) heavy cream

½ cup (50 g) powdered sugar, plus more for dusting

1 tsp pure vanilla extract

8 oz (225 g) mascarpone cheese

About 1¼ cups (355 g) blackberry jam

To make the crepes, in a blender, combine the milk, eggs, water, butter, flour, sugar, and salt and blend until smooth and thoroughly mixed. Pour the batter through a fine-mesh sieve into a glass jar and refrigerate for at least 2 hours or up to overnight.

Heat a 9-inch (23-cm) crepe pan or nonstick frying pan over medium-high heat. Brush lightly with melted butter. Gently stir the crepe batter.

For each crepe, pour a scant ¼ cup (60 ml) of the batter into the pan, quickly tilting and swirling the pan to coat the bottom with the batter. Use a small metal spatula to help spread and smooth the batter quickly.

Cook until the center of the crepe bubbles and the edges begin to dry, about 30 seconds. Using a thin, flat spatula, flip the crepe and cook until golden on the second side, about 20 seconds. Transfer the crepe to a plate. Repeat with the remaining batter, brushing with butter as needed before cooking each crepe. Stack the crepes on the plate. You should have about 10 crepes.

To make the filling, in a bowl, beat together the heavy cream, powdered sugar, and vanilla until medium-stiff peaks form. Put the mascarpone in another bowl. Gently fold the whipped cream into the mascarpone until combined. Let stand for 5 minutes to thicken slightly.

To assemble, spoon some of the mascarpone filling down the center of a crepe and roll up the crepe. Repeat with the remaining crepes and filling. Divide the crepes among plates, dust with powdered sugar, and serve with a spoonful of the jam.

BANANA DULCE DE LECHE WAFFLES

MAKES 4 SERVINGS

1 cup (240 ml) dulce de leche

2½ cups (600 ml) whole milk, or as needed

4 tbsp (60 g) unsalted butter

2 large eggs, separated

1 tsp pure vanilla extract

2 cups (250 g) all-purpose flour

3 tbsp sugar

4 tsp baking powder

¼ tsp kosher salt

2 ripe bananas, peeled and thinly sliced

Avocado oil or canola oil for cooking

These brown butter and banana waffles make the ideal base for drizzles of rich-sweet dulce de leche. For plain waffles, simply omit the bananas and serve pure maple syrup or your favorite fruit compote alongside. The keys to achieving crispy results are using a preheated waffle iron and patience (no peeking!). Freeze any leftover waffles in an airtight container, then rewarm in a toaster.

In a small saucepan, warm the dulce de leche over medium heat, stirring frequently, until melted. Gradually whisk in about ½ cup (120 ml) of the milk, or enough to make a pourable sauce about the thickness of heavy cream. Remove from the heat, cover, and keep warm.

In another small saucepan, melt the butter over medium-low heat. Cook, stirring occasionally, until the milk solids in the bottom of the pan turn a toasty brown, about 3 minutes. Transfer to a bowl and let cool slightly. Add the remaining 2 cups (475 ml) of milk, the egg yolks, and the vanilla and whisk until combined.

In a large bowl, sift together the flour, sugar, baking powder, and salt. Add the milk–egg yolk mixture and whisk just until combined (a few lumps are okay). Gently fold in the bananas. In a medium bowl, using an electric mixer, beat the egg whites on high speed until soft peaks form. Scoop the egg whites over the batter and gently and evenly fold in the whites.

Using a paper towel, lightly oil the grid of a waffle iron with oil, then preheat the iron. Following the manufacturer's instructions, ladle some of the batter onto the grid of the waffle iron, close the lid, and cook until the waffle is golden brown and crisp and steam is no longer escaping from the sides of the iron. The timing will depend on the iron.

Transfer to a plate and serve right away, or place on a baking sheet in a 200°F (95°C) oven for up to 20 minutes before serving. Repeat with the remaining batter, being careful not to stack the waffles on the sheet. Serve the waffles drizzled with the dulce de leche sauce.

FRIED CHICKEN WITH CORNMEAL WAFFLES

With their boxy pockets and a crisp exterior, waffles capture syrups, sauces, and chunky toppings. This cornmeal version is the perfect partner for juicy fried chicken. Serve these with plenty of honey or pure maple syrup, butter, and hot pepper sauce. Keep both the chicken and the waffles warm in a low oven to give you time to make everything and serve it all together.

MAKES 4 SERVINGS

FOR THE FRIED CHICKEN

⅔ cup (90 g) all-purpose flour

½ tsp baking powder

½ tsp kosher salt

½ tsp freshly ground pepper

⅔ cup (160 ml) buttermilk

4 boneless, skinless chicken breast halves (about 170 g each)

Avocado oil or canola oil for deep-frying

FOR THE CORNMEAL WAFFLES

1½ cups (200 g) fine yellow cornmeal

¾ cup (90 g) all-purpose flour

2 tbsp sugar

2 tsp baking powder

1 tsp baking soda

½ tsp kosher salt

2 cups (475 ml) buttermilk

6 tbsp (90 g) unsalted butter, melted, plus butter for serving

2 large eggs, separated

Avocado oil or canola oil for cooking

Honey or pure maple syrup for serving

Hot pepper sauce for serving

To make the fried chicken, in a shallow bowl, whisk together the flour, baking powder, salt, and pepper until combined. Pour the buttermilk into another shallow bowl. Using a meat pounder, pound the chicken breast halves until they are a uniform ½ inch (12 mm) thick. One at a time, dip the chicken into the buttermilk, letting the excess liquid drip back into the bowl, then coat the chicken with the seasoned flour, shaking off the excess. Transfer to a rimmed baking sheet.

Place a wire rack over another rimmed baking sheet and set near the stove. Preheat the oven to 200°F (95°C). Pour oil to a depth of ½ inch (12 mm) into a large cast-iron or other heavy frying pan and heat over high heat to 375°F (190°C) on a deep-frying thermometer.

In batches if necessary, add the chicken to the hot oil and cook, turning once, until golden brown and an instant-read thermometer inserted in the thickest part reads 165°F (74°C), about 8 minutes. Adjust the heat as needed so the oil stays at 375°F (190°C). Using tongs, transfer the chicken to the rack to drain. Keep warm in the oven.

Meanwhile, make the waffles. Preheat a waffle iron. In a large bowl, sift together the cornmeal, flour, sugar, baking powder, baking soda, and salt. In a medium bowl, whisk together the buttermilk with the melted butter and egg yolks. Add the buttermilk mixture to the cornmeal mixture and stir until just combined (the batter will be lumpy). In a small bowl, using a clean whisk or a handheld mixer on high speed, beat the egg whites until soft peaks form. Scoop the whites over the batter and gently fold them in evenly.

Using a paper towel, lightly oil the grid of a waffle iron with oil, then preheat the iron. Following the manufacturer's instructions, ladle some of the batter onto the grid of the waffle iron, close the lid, and cook until the waffle is golden brown and crisp and steam is no longer escaping from the sides of the iron. The timing will depend on the iron.

Serve the chicken and waffles hot with butter, honey, and hot pepper sauce passed on the side.

MATCHA-GLAZED BUTTERMILK DOUGHNUTS

Nothing beats a fresh doughnut, and they are never fresher than those you make at home. Here, the glaze features matcha, an earthy green tea powder used to flavor all sorts of desserts and drinks. You can skip the glaze and turn these into spiced buttermilk doughnuts by adding 1 tsp cinnamon and ¼ tsp nutmeg to the dough, then tossing the warm doughnuts in cinnamon-sugar.

MAKES 8 DOUGHNUTS

FOR THE DOUGHNUTS

2¼ cups (285 g) all-purpose flour, plus more for dusting

½ tsp baking powder

½ tsp baking soda

½ tsp kosher salt

1 large egg

½ cup (100 g) granulated sugar

½ cup (120 ml) buttermilk

1 tbsp unsalted butter, melted

2 tsp pure vanilla extract

Avocado oil or canola oil for deep-frying

FOR THE MATCHA GLAZE

2 cups (225 g) powdered sugar, sifted, plus more as needed

1 tsp matcha powder

¼ cup (60 ml) whole milk, plus more as needed

1 tsp pure vanilla extract

Pinch kosher salt

To make the doughnuts, in a small bowl, sift together the flour, baking powder, baking soda, and salt. Set aside.

In a large bowl, whisk together the egg and granulated sugar until creamy and pale. Add the buttermilk, melted butter, and vanilla and whisk until blended. Add the flour mixture and mix with a wooden spoon until the dough holds together.

Line a platter with paper towels. Pour oil to a depth of 2 inches (5 cm) into a deep, heavy saucepan and heat to 365°F (185°C) on a deep-frying thermometer. Turn the dough out onto a lightly floured work surface. Roll out into a 9-inch (23-cm) circle about ½ inch (12 mm) thick. Use a 2¾-inch (7-cm) biscuit cutter to cut out circles, then use a ½-inch (12-mm) cutter to cut a circle from the center of each. Alternatively, use a doughnut cutter.

When the oil is hot, place 2 doughnuts and 2 doughnut holes into the oil and fry until deep golden brown, about 2 minutes. Using a slotted spoon, turn and fry on the second side, about 1½ minutes. Using the slotted spoon, transfer to the prepared platter to drain. Repeat with the remaining doughnuts and doughnut holes, allowing the oil to return to 365°F (185°C) between batches.

To make the glaze, in a wide, shallow bowl, whisk together the powdered sugar and matcha. Add the milk, vanilla, and salt and whisk until smooth and well blended. Add more milk, 1 tsp at a time, if needed for a thinner consistency, or add more powdered sugar if the mixture is too thin.

When the doughnuts and holes are cool enough to handle but are still warm, dip the tops in the glaze, letting any excess fall back into the bowl. Place on a wire rack until the glaze sets, about 30 minutes, then serve.

Maple Glaze + Bacon

Strawberry Glaze + Confetti Sprinkles

Raspberry Glaze + Freeze-Dried Raspberries

Lavender Glaze + Candied Violets

Cinnamon + Sugar

Lemon Glaze + Zest

Chocolate Glaze + Toasted Shaved Coconut

Rose-Tinted Vanilla Glaze + Fresh Edible Blossoms

RAISED GLAZED DOUGHNUTS

MAKES 8 DOUGHNUTS

1 cup (240 ml) whole milk, warm (110°F/43°C)

1 package (2¼ tsp) instant yeast

3 cups (370 g) all-purpose flour, plus more for dusting

¼ cup (50 g) sugar

3 tbsp vegetable shortening, melted and cooled slightly

1 large egg

2 tsp kosher salt

Avocado oil or canola oil for greasing and frying

Glaze of choice (see next page)

Sprinkles or other toppings (optional)

Few morning treats start off the day with more promise than a gorgeously glazed and decorated doughnut. Keep in mind that the dough takes a couple of hours to rise, but once it's ready, the frying part is easier than you might think. Set out glazes and sprinkles and let everyone customize their doughnuts as they please.

Pour the warm milk into a small bowl, sprinkle the yeast on top, and stir gently. Let stand in a warm spot until foamy, 5–10 minutes.

Transfer the yeast mixture to the bowl of a stand mixer fitted with the paddle attachment. Add 1½ cups (185 g) of the flour, the sugar, shortening, egg, and salt and beat on low speed until combined, about 2 minutes. Add the remaining 1½ cups (185 g) flour, raise the speed to medium, and beat until incorporated, about 30 seconds. Switch to the dough hook and knead on medium speed until the dough is smooth and pulls away from the bowl, 3–4 minutes. Oil a large bowl. Transfer the dough to the bowl and cover with a kitchen towel. Let the dough rise in a warm spot until doubled in size, about 1 hour.

Punch down the dough, turn out onto a floured work surface, and roll out ½ inch (12 mm) thick. Using a doughnut cutter or 2 different-size round cutters (3½ inch/9 cm and 1 inch/2.5 cm), cut out doughnuts and holes. Transfer to a floured baking sheet, cover with a kitchen towel, and let rise in a warm spot until doubled in size, about 1 hour.

Meanwhile, make the glaze or prepare the sugar coating of your choice. Set aside.

Pour oil to a depth of 2 inches (5 cm) into a deep fryer or deep, heavy sauté pan (do not fill more than half full) and warm over medium-high heat until it registers 360°F (182°C) on a deep-frying thermometer. Line a baking sheet with paper towels.

Carefully lower 2–5 doughnuts or holes into the hot oil and deep-fry until dark golden, about 1½ minutes. Using tongs, turn and cook until dark golden on the second side, about 1 minute longer. Transfer to the prepared baking sheet. Fry the remaining doughnuts and holes, allowing the oil to return to 360°F (182°C) between batches.

When the doughnuts and holes are cool enough to handle but are still warm, dip the tops in the glaze or coating, letting any excess fall back into the bowl. Decorate with sprinkles or other toppings (if using). Place on a wire rack until the glaze sets, about 30 minutes, then serve.

Basic Glaze

MAKES ABOUT ¾ CUP (180 ML)

2 cups (225 g) powdered sugar

¼ cup (60 ml) whole milk, plus more if needed

1½ tsp pure vanilla extract or other extract such as lavender, raspberry, or coconut

¼ tsp kosher salt

2–3 drops food coloring (optional)

In a bowl, stir together the powdered sugar, milk, vanilla, and salt until smooth and well blended. Add more milk, 1 tsp at a time, if needed for a thinner consistency. If a tinted glaze is desired, stir in food coloring until blended. Use right away.

Chocolate Glaze

MAKES ABOUT 1⅓ CUPS (325 ML)

¼ cup (60 ml) hot water

¼ lb (115 g) semisweet chocolate

2 cups (225 g) powdered sugar

5 tbsp (70 g) unsalted butter

1½ tsp pure vanilla extract

¼ tsp kosher salt

In a heatproof bowl set over but not touching barely simmering water in a saucepan, combine the hot water, chocolate, powdered sugar, butter, vanilla, and salt. Cook, stirring occasionally, until the chocolate and butter are melted, 2–3 minutes. Remove from the heat and stir until smooth and well blended. Use right away.

Strawberry Glaze

MAKES ABOUT 1 CUP (240 ML)

2 cups (225 g) powdered sugar

½ cup (140 g) strawberry jelly thinned with 2 tbsp water

Pinch kosher salt

In a bowl, stir together the powdered sugar, strawberry jelly, and salt until smooth and well blended. Use right away.

Maple Glaze

MAKES ABOUT ½ CUP (120 ML)

1¾ cups (200 g) powdered sugar

3 tbsp whole milk

2 tsp pure maple extract

In a bowl, stir together the powdered sugar, milk, and maple extract until smooth and well blended. Use right away.

Lemon Glaze

MAKES ABOUT ⅔ CUP (160 ML)

½ cup (120 g) plain whole-milk Greek or regular yogurt

Grated zest of 1 lemon

¼ tsp kosher salt

1 cup (115 g) powdered sugar

In a bowl, stir together the yogurt, lemon zest, and salt. Add the powdered sugar and stir until smooth and well blended. Use right away.

LEMON-RICOTTA PANCAKES WITH BLUEBERRY COMPOTE

MAKES 4 SERVINGS

FOR THE BLUEBERRY COMPOTE

3 cups (425 g) blueberries

½ cup (155 g) pure maple syrup

2 cups (450 g) whole-milk ricotta cheese

⅓ cup (40 g) all-purpose flour

3 large eggs, separated

3 tbsp sugar

2 tbsp unsalted butter, melted

Grated zest of 1 lemon

1 tsp pure vanilla extract

Avocado oil or canola oil for cooking

These lighter-than-air pancakes get their delicate texture from the addition of whipped eggs whites and ricotta cheese. You can omit the lemon zest if you like, although it pairs wonderfully with the blueberry compote. For a mixed berry compote, use equal amounts of blackberries, raspberries, and blueberries.

To make the compote, in a saucepan, combine the blueberries and maple syrup. Place over medium heat and cook, stirring occasionally, just until the berries begin to release some juices, about 3 minutes. Set aside.

In a bowl, whisk together the ricotta, flour, egg yolks, sugar, melted butter, lemon zest, and vanilla. In another bowl, using an electric mixer, beat the egg whites on high speed until soft peaks form. Gently and evenly fold the egg whites into the batter.

Heat a griddle or large frying pan over medium heat until hot. Lightly oil the griddle. For each pancake, pour about ¼ cup (60 ml) of the batter onto the griddle and cook until bubbles form on the surface, about 1½ minutes. Turn the pancakes and cook until golden on the second sides, about 1 minute. Transfer to a platter. Repeat until all the batter is used, oiling the griddle as needed.

Serve the pancakes with the blueberry compote on the side.

NECTARINE OVEN PANCAKE

MAKES 4 SERVINGS

⅔ cup (160 ml) whole milk

⅔ cup (90 g) all-purpose flour

¼ tsp kosher salt

3 large eggs

4 tbsp (60 g) unsalted butter, melted

3 ripe nectarines, halved, pitted, and sliced

2 tbsp firmly packed light brown sugar

2 tsp fresh lemon juice

Powdered sugar for dusting

Whipped cream for serving (optional)

Also known as a Dutch Baby or a German pancake, these impressive skillet pancakes puff up like a giant popover in the oven. Once baked, the buttery shell can be filled with all sorts of fruit—nectarines or peaches are exceptional, as are sautéed apples or pears, or a mixture of berries. If you like, top the pancakes with ¼ cup (20 g) toasted sliced almonds.

Place a 12-inch (30-cm) ovenproof frying pan in the oven and preheat the oven to 425°F (220°C).

To make the batter, in a blender, combine the milk, flour, salt, and eggs and blend until smooth. With the motor running, drizzle in 1 tbsp of the melted butter and blend until incorporated.

Remove the hot frying pan from the oven. Using a pastry brush, brush 1 tbsp of the melted butter all over the bottom and sides of the pan. Working quickly, pour in the batter and transfer the pan to the oven. Bake until the pancake is puffed and golden, and golden, 15–20 minutes.

Meanwhile, make the peach filling. In another large frying pan over medium heat, warm the remaining 2 tbsp butter. Add the nectarines, brown sugar, and lemon juice and cook, stirring occasionally, until the nectarines release their juices and the brown sugar dissolves, about 3 minutes. Remove from the heat.

Remove the pan from the oven. Pour the nectarine compote onto the pancake. Dust lightly with powdered sugar. Serve with whipped cream (if using).

PANCAKES

Fluffy, feather-light pancakes are easy to achieve if you follow a few basic tips. First, use fresh, good-quality ingredients. Next, don't overmix the ibatter; stir it only until the wet and dry ingredients are incorporated. And finally, cook the pancakes on a preheated, well-greased, and well-seasoned surface. Here are three basic pancake recipes followed by an array of mix-ins and topping ideas.

Fluffy Buttermilk Pancakes

1½ cups (185 g) all-purpose flour

1½ tsp baking powder

¾ tsp baking soda

¼ tsp kosher salt

2 large eggs

2 cups (475 ml) buttermilk

3 tbsp unsalted butter, melted, plus more for cooking

In a large bowl, stir together the flour, baking powder, baking soda, and salt. In a medium bowl, whisk together the eggs, buttermilk, and melted butter. Add the egg mixture to the flour mixture and stir until incorporated. (The batter will be slightly lumpy.)

Heat a griddle or a large frying pan over medium heat. Coat generously with melted butter and then ladle about ⅓ cup (80 ml) of batter onto the griddle for each pancake. Cook until the edges are golden and bubbles form on the surface, then flip the pancakes and continue cooking until cooked through, about 3 minutes total. Keep warm while you cook the remaining pancakes. Serve hot.

Whole-Grain Pancakes

1 cup (115 g) whole-wheat flour

½ cup (60 g) all-purpose flour

½ cup (50 g) rolled oats

2 tbsp firmly packed dark brown sugar

1½ tsp baking powder

¾ tsp baking soda

¼ tsp kosher salt

2 large eggs

2 cups (475 ml) buttermilk

3 tbsp unsalted butter, melted, plus more for cooking

In a large bowl, stir together both flours, oats, brown sugar, baking powder, baking soda, and salt. In a medium bowl, whisk together the eggs, buttermilk, and melted butter. Add the egg mixture to the flour mixture and stir until incorporated. (The batter will be slightly lumpy.)

Heat a griddle or a large frying pan over medium heat. Coat generously with melted butter and then ladle about ⅓ cup (80 ml) batter onto the griddle for each pancake. Cook until the edges are golden and bubbles form on the surface, then flip the pancakes and continue cooking until cooked through, about 3 minutes total. Keep warm while you cook the remaining pancakes. Serve hot.

Gluten-Free Pancakes

2 cups (225 g) gluten-free
all-purpose flour

2 tbsp sugar

4 tsp baking powder

½ tsp salt

2 large eggs

2 cups (475 ml) buttermilk

⅓ cup (80 ml) whole milk, at room
temperature, plus more as needed

3 tbsp unsalted butter, melted,
plus more for cooking

In a large bowl, stir together the gluten-free flour, sugar, baking powder, and salt. In a medium bowl, whisk together the eggs, buttermilk, milk, and melted butter. Add the egg mixture to the flour mixture and stir until incorporated.

Heat a griddle or a large frying pan over medium-low heat. Coat generously with melted butter and then ladle slightly less than ¼ cup (60 ml) batter onto the griddle for each pancake. Cook without moving until the top looks dry, bubbles are breaking the entire surface, and the bottom is deeply golden brown, about 4 minutes. Flip the pancakes and continue cooking until deep golden brown and cooked through, about 5 minutes longer. Keep warm while you cook the remaining pancakes. (The batter will thicken as it stands, so add more milk or water as needed, about 1 tbsp at a time, stirring regularly.) Serve the pancakes hot.

PANCAKE BATTER MIX-INS

½ cup (60 g) raspberries + ¼ cup
(40 g) white chocolate chips

½ cup (60 g) diced bananas + ¼ cup
(40 g) mini chocolate chips

½ cup (90 g) finely chopped drained
pineapple + 3 tbsp toasted coconut
(page 158)

½ cup (60 g) blueberries + 2 tsp
grated lemon zest

½ cup (80 g) sautéed diced apples +
½ tsp ground cinnamon

2 tsp pumpkin pie spice

PANCAKE TOPPINGS

Blueberry compote (page 55) + sweetened whipped cream

Quick strawberry jam (page 73) + sliced toasted almonds (page 158)

Dulce de leche + ¼ cup (30 g) chopped toasted pecans (page 158)

Peanut or almond butter + diced bananas + honey

Diced fresh pineapple + macadamia nuts + toasted coconut (page 158)

Sliced ripe peaches + powdered sugar

Strawberry syrup + fresh strawberries + whipped cream + shaved chocolate

Sautéed apples or pears + maple syrup

SWEET POTATO PANCAKES WITH PECANS AND BROWN-SUGAR SAUCE

MAKES 4–6 SERVINGS

2 sweet potatoes, scrubbed

¾ cup (175 g) unsalted butter, at room temperature, plus more for serving

1 cup (210 g) plus 2 tbsp firmly packed light brown sugar

¼ cup (60 ml) water

1½ cups (360 ml) whole milk, plus more as needed

2 large eggs

1½ tsp pure vanilla extract

¾ cup (90 g) whole-wheat flour

¾ cup (90 g) all-purpose flour

1 tbsp baking powder

½ tsp ground cinnamon

½ tsp freshly grated nutmeg

½ tsp fine sea salt

Avocado oil or canola oil for cooking

½ cup (60 g) pecans, toasted (page 158) and coarsely chopped

Sweet potatoes add tenderness and flavor to these warmly spiced, Southern-style pancakes. Served with a brown sugar sauce and chopped toasted pecans, the pancakes are reminiscent of both pecan and sweet potato pies. To save time, prepare the baked sweet potato and the brown sugar sauce in advance.

Preheat the oven to 400°F (200°C). Pierce the sweet potatoes a few times with a fork, place on a rimmed baking sheet, and bake until tender, about 1 hour. (Alternatively, microwave the sweet potatoes on high until tender, about 8 minutes.) Split each sweet potato lengthwise and let cool until just easy to handle, then scoop out and reserve 1¼ cups (170 g) of the flesh.

Meanwhile, in a medium saucepan, melt ½ cup (115 g) of the butter over medium heat. Add 1 cup (210 g) of the brown sugar and whisk until melted. Whisk in the water and bring to a simmer. Reduce the heat to low and simmer until the sauce has reduced slightly, 8–10 minutes. Remove from the heat and cover to keep warm.

Reduce the oven heat to 200°F (95°C). In a food processor, combine the reserved warm sweet potato flesh and the remaining 4 tbsp (60 g) butter and process until the butter is fully incorporated. Add ½ cup (120 ml) of the milk, the eggs, the remaining 2 tbsp brown sugar, and the vanilla, and process until smooth. Transfer to a bowl and whisk in the remaining 1 cup (240 ml) milk.

In a large bowl, sift together both flours, the baking powder, cinnamon, nutmeg, and salt. Pour the sweet potato mixture into the flour mixture and stir until just combined. Do not overmix.

Place a griddle or large frying pan over medium heat until hot. Lightly oil the griddle. For each pancake, pour about ¼ cup (60 ml) of the batter onto the griddle and cook until bubbles form and break on the surface, about 2½ minutes. Flip the pancakes and cook until the other sides are golden brown, about 2 minutes longer. Transfer to a baking sheet and keep warm in the oven. Repeat until all the batter is used, oiling the griddle as needed. If the batter begins to thicken, thin it with a bit more milk.

Whisk the reserved sauce well and pour into a serving pitcher. Serve the pancakes piping hot, sprinkled with the pecans. Pass the warm sauce and butter on the side.

SAVORY BACON, CHEDDAR & GREEN ONION PANCAKES

MAKES 6 SERVINGS

1½ cups (200 g) fine white
or yellow cornmeal

1 tsp kosher salt

1 tsp sugar

1½ cups (350 ml) boiling water

¼–½ cup (60–120 ml) whole milk

⅓ cup finely chopped cooked bacon
(3–4 slices)

3 green onions, white and green parts,
finely chopped

½ cup (60 g) shredded
Cheddar cheese

Freshly ground pepper

Avocado oil or canola oil for cooking

Sour cream for garnish

The crunch of cornmeal gives these savory pancakes an appealing texture and a bit of heft. Embellished with salty bits of bacon, sharp Cheddar cheese, and chopped green onions, they're excellent served with a dollop of sour cream. For a sweeter take, omit the onions and drizzle the pancakes with honey.

Preheat the oven to 250°F (120°C).

In a large bowl, whisk together the cornmeal, salt, and sugar. Slowly and carefully stir in the boiling water, whisking until smooth and quite stiff. Let the batter stand for 5 minutes. Stir in enough of the milk to make a batter with the consistency of porridge. Stir in the bacon, green onions, and cheese, then season with pepper.

Heat a griddle or large frying pan over medium heat until hot. Lightly oil the griddle. For each pancake, pour about ¼ cup (60 ml) of the batter onto the griddle. Flatten the cakes with a spatula so they cook evenly. Cook until browned and crisp, 5–7 minutes. Using the spatula, carefully turn the pancakes and cook until browned and crisp on the second sides, 5–7 minutes. Do not let the pancakes cook too quickly; the insides should remain a bit moist. Transfer to an ovenproof platter and place in the oven to keep warm; do not cover the pancakes or they will get soggy. Repeat until all the batter is used, oiling the griddle as needed.

Serve the pancakes with a dollop of sour cream.

POTATO LATKES WITH SOUR CREAM & APPLESAUCE

MAKES 6 SERVINGS

2 lb (1 kg) russet potatoes, peeled

½ yellow onion, grated

2 large eggs, lightly beaten

2 tbsp sour cream, plus more for serving

¾ tsp kosher salt

¼ tsp freshly ground pepper

Avocado oil or canola oil for frying

2 cups (450 g) applesauce

These irresistible, crisp-edged potato pancakes are traditionally paired with sour cream and applesauce. For a heartier version, top the latkes with a poached egg. They're also delicious garnished with creme fraîche or sour cream, smoked salmon, and chopped chives.

Preheat the oven to 250°F (120°C).

Shred the potatoes on the coarsest holes of a box grater. Enclose half of the grated potatoes in a kitchen towel and twist the towel to press out as much liquid as possible. Transfer to a large bowl. Repeat with the remaining grated potatoes. Add the onion, eggs, sour cream, salt, and pepper to the bowl and stir to combine.

Line an ovenproof platter with paper towels. Pour oil to a depth of ¼ inch (6 mm) into a heavy frying pan and heat over medium heat to 365°F (185°C) on a deep-frying thermometer.

For each latke, ladle ¼ cup (60 ml) of the potato mixture onto the hot surface. Cook the latkes until browned and crisp, about 2 minutes. Using a slotted spoon, carefully turn the latkes and cook until browned and crisp on the second sides, about 2 minutes. Using the slotted spoon, transfer to the prepared platter and place in the oven to keep warm; do not cover the latkes or they will get soggy. Repeat with the remaining potato mixture to make about 18 latkes. The latkes can be kept warm in the oven for 20 minutes.

Serve with more sour cream and the applesauce.

SWEET & SAVORY BREADS

Pistachio-Orange Sticky Buns 67

Cacio e Pepe Mini Scones 68

Pumpkin Coffee Cake with Pecan Streusel 69

Overnight Cinnamon Rolls with Cream Cheese Icing 70

Spiced Apple Cider Mini Doughnut Muffins 72

Cream-Currant Scones with Quick Strawberry Jam 73

Raspberry-Lemon Streusel Muffins 75

Lemon–Poppy Seed Drizzle Bread 76

Buttermilk Biscuits 77

Breakfast Fruit Puffs 78

Savory Mushroom & Goat Cheese Twists 85

Herb & Olive Focaccia 86

Cheddar-Jalapeño Cornbread 87

PISTACHIO-ORANGE STICKY BUNS

MAKES 18 STICKY BUNS

FOR THE DOUGH

¾ cup (180 ml) whole milk, warm (110°F/43°C)

1 package (2¼ tsp) instant yeast

4 tbsp (50 g) granulated sugar

4½ cups (570 g) all-purpose flour, plus more for dusting

4 large eggs

1½ tsp kosher salt

½ tsp ground cinnamon

¼ tsp ground cardamom

6 tbsp (90 g) unsalted butter, at room temperature, cut into chunks

FOR THE CARAMEL

1¼ cups (270 g) firmly packed light brown sugar

¼ cup (90 g) runny honey

½ cup (115 g) unsalted butter, melted

6 oz (170 g) coarsely chopped pistachios

¼ tsp kosher salt

FOR THE FILLING

¾ cup (140 g) granulated sugar

2 tsp ground cinnamon

½ tsp ground cardamom

Grated zest of 1 small orange

3 tbsp unsalted butter, melted and cooled

It's hard to resist the decadent and gooey appeal of sticky buns, which are traditionally made with chopped toasted pecans. In this version, a cinnamon-cardamom dough encases a spiced sugar filling aromatic with orange zest, while pistachios replace the pecans in a honey-sweetened caramel.

To make the dough, in the bowl of a stand mixer, combine the milk, yeast, and 2 tbsp of the granulated sugar. Let stand until foamy, about 10 minutes. Add the flour, the remaining 2 tbsp sugar, the eggs, salt, cinnamon, and cardamom. Attach the dough hook and knead on low speed until the ingredients come together. Add the butter and knead until the dough is smooth and springy, about 7 minutes.

Lightly oil a large bowl. Form the dough into a ball, put it in the oiled bowl, and cover the bowl with plastic wrap. Let the dough rise at room temperature until it doubles, 1½–2 hours.

Butter two 9-inch (23-cm) round cake pans.

To make the caramel, in a medium bowl, stir together the brown sugar, honey, melted butter, pistachios, and salt. Spread half of the pistachio mixture into each prepared pan in an even layer. Set aside.

Punch down the dough and dump onto a floured work surface. Cut it in half. Roll out each half into a 9-by-14-inch (23-by-35-cm) rectangle. Position the rectangles horizontally.

To make the filling, in a small bowl, stir together the granulated sugar, cinnamon, cardamom, and orange zest. Spread each rectangle with half of the melted butter, then sprinkle each with half of the sugar mixture, leaving ½ inch (12 mm) of the side closest to you uncovered. Starting at the side farthest from you, roll up the rectangle into a log. Pinch the seams to seal. The log should be about 14 inches (35 cm) long.

Cut each log crosswise into 9 equal slices. Arrange the slices, cut side up, in the pans. Cover the pans loosely with plastic wrap and let stand in a warm, draft-free spot until puffy, about 1 hour, or refrigerate overnight, then let stand at room temperature until puffy, 1–2 hours, before baking.

Preheat the oven to 350°F (180°C). Bake until the buns are golden brown and cooked through, 35–40 minutes. Let cool in the pans on a wire rack for 5 minutes, then carefully invert each pan onto a plate and unmold the buns. When they are still warm but cool enough to handle, pull them apart and dig in.

CACIO E PEPE MINI SCONES

**MAKES ABOUT
24 MINI SCONES**

2 cups (250 g) all-purpose flour,
plus more for dusting

2 tsp baking powder

1 cup (115 g) grated pecorino cheese

Pinch of kosher salt

1 tsp coarsely ground pepper

½ cup (115 g) cold unsalted butter,
cut into chunks

1 large egg

¾ cup (180 ml) plus 1 tbsp
heavy cream

Cheese scones are great, but cacio e pepe scones—a riff on the beloved Roman pasta dish—are exceptional. Salty pecorino and plenty of black pepper imbue these savory bite-size treats with a lot of flavor. They are perfect paired with egg dishes or a fresh salad, or just eaten right out of the oven.

Position a rack in the upper third of the oven and preheat to 400°F (200°C). Line a rimmed baking sheet with parchment paper.

In a food processor, combine the flour, baking powder, cheese, salt, and pepper and pulse briefly to mix. Add the butter and pulse until the mixture looks like coarse bread crumbs. In a small bowl, whisk together the egg and cream until blended. Pour the egg mixture into the processor and pulse just until the dough comes together.

Dump the dough onto a lightly floured work surface and press together, folding the dough over onto itself a few times. Press it out into a flat disk. Using a floured rolling pin, roll out the dough about ½ inch (12 mm) thick. Using a 1¾-inch (4.5-cm) biscuit cutter, cut out as many scones as you can. Gather up the scraps, press together, roll out again, and cut out more scones.

Space the scones evenly on the prepared baking sheet. Bake until the scones are golden, 13–15 minutes. Let cool slightly on a wire rack before serving.

PUMPKIN COFFEE CAKE WITH PECAN STREUSEL

The rich flavor of pumpkin and warm spices plus a thick layer of crunchy brown sugar and pecan streusel make this an ideal addition to any holiday or autumn brunch table. If you prefer, omit the pecans or swap them out for lightly toasted walnuts.

MAKES ONE 9-INCH (23-CM) COFFEE CAKE; SERVES 8–10

FOR THE STREUSEL
⅓ cup (40 g) all-purpose flour

½ cup (100 g) firmly packed light brown sugar

1 tsp ground cinnamon

¼ tsp kosher salt

6 tbsp (90 g) unsalted butter, melted

1 cup (115 g) chopped pecans, lightly toasted (page 158)

FOR THE COFFEE CAKE
1½ cups (185 g) all-purpose flour

2 tsp baking powder

½ tsp baking soda

2 tsp ground cinnamon

1 tsp ground ginger

¼ tsp freshly grated nutmeg

½ tsp kosher salt

½ cup (115 g) unsalted butter, at room temperature

1 cup (210 g) firmly packed light brown sugar

2 large eggs

½ cup (120 ml) pumpkin puree

½ cup (115 g) sour cream

FOR THE GLAZE (OPTIONAL)
½ cup (50 g) powdered sugar, sifted

1 tsp whole milk

1 tsp pure vanilla extract

Preheat the oven to 350°F (180°C). Butter and flour a 9-inch (23-cm) springform pan.

To make the streusel, in a medium bowl, combine the flour, brown sugar, cinnamon, and salt. Drizzle with the melted butter and stir with a fork until the mixture looks like coarse crumbs. Stir in the pecans until well combined. Set aside.

To make the coffee cake, in a medium bowl, sift together the flour, baking powder, baking soda, cinnamon, ginger, nutmeg, and salt. Set aside.

In the bowl of a stand mixer fitted with the paddle attachment, beat together the butter and brown sugar on medium-high speed until well combined. Beat in the eggs, one at a time, stopping the mixer to scrape down the sides of the bowl with a rubber spatula. Add the pumpkin puree and sour cream and mix with the spatula. Stir in the flour mixture. The batter will be quite thick.

Spread half of the batter in the prepared pan. Sprinkle half of the streusel over the batter. Dollop the remaining batter over the streusel and gently spread the batter in an even layer. Sprinkle with the remaining streusel.

Bake until a toothpick inserted into the center of the cake comes out clean, about 50 minutes. Transfer the pan to a wire rack and let cool for about 30 minutes. Remove the sides from the pan and slide the cake onto the rack.

If making the glaze, in a small bowl, whisk together the powdered sugar, milk, and vanilla. Drizzle over the top of the cooled cake. Cut into thick wedges and serve.

OVERNIGHT CINNAMON ROLLS WITH CREAM CHEESE ICING

Is there anything better than waking up on a weekend morning with the aroma of these big, puffy rolls baking in the oven? Fragrant with cinnamon and brown sugar, the irresistible rolls are topped with rich cream cheese icing. For easy variations, sprinkle ½ cup (90 g) raisins or currants and/or ½ cup (60 g) chopped pecans over the filling before rolling up the dough.

MAKES 10–12 CINNAMON ROLLS

FOR THE DOUGH

¾ cup (180 ml) whole milk, warm (110°F/43°C)

1 package (2¼ tsp) instant yeast

¼ cup (50 g) granulated sugar

4½ cups (570 g) all-purpose flour, plus more for dusting

4 large eggs

1½ tsp kosher salt

½ tsp ground cinnamon

6 tbsp (90 g) unsalted butter, at room temperature, cut into chunks

FOR THE FILLING

¾ cup (155 g) firmly packed light brown sugar

1 tbsp ground cinnamon

3 tbsp unsalted butter, melted and cooled

1 egg beaten with 1 tsp water, for egg wash

FOR THE CREAM CHEESE ICING

2 oz (60 g) cream cheese, at room temperature

2 tbsp unsalted butter, at room temperature

½ tsp pure vanilla extract

1½ cups (170 g) powdered sugar

3–4 tbsp whole milk

To make the dough, in the bowl of a stand mixer, combine the milk, yeast, and 2 tbsp of the granulated sugar. Let stand until foamy, about 10 minutes. Add the flour, the remaining 2 tbsp sugar, the eggs, salt, and cinnamon. Attach the dough hook and knead on low speed until the ingredients come together. Add the butter and knead until the dough is smooth and springy, about 7 minutes.

Lightly oil a large bowl. Form the dough into a ball, put it in the oiled bowl, and cover the bowl with plastic wrap. Let the dough rise at room temperature until it doubles, 1½–2 hours.

Generously butter a 9-by-13-inch (23-by-33-cm) baking dish. Punch down the dough and dump onto a floured work surface. Cut it in half. Roll out each half into a 9-by-14-inch (23-by-35-cm) rectangle. Position the rectangles horizontally.

To make the filling, in a small bowl, stir together the brown sugar and cinnamon. Spread each rectangle with half of the melted butter, then sprinkle each with half of the sugar mixture, leaving ½ inch (12 mm) of the side closest to you uncovered. Starting at the side farthest from you, roll up the rectangle into a log. Pinch the seams to seal. The logs should be about 14 inches (35 cm) long.

Cut each log crosswise into 8 equal slices. Arrange the slices, cut side up, in the prepared dish with even space between them. Cover the dish loosely with plastic wrap, transfer to the refrigerator, and let rise overnight. The next morning, let the rolls stand at room temperature until puffy, 1–2 hours, before baking. (Alternatively, leave out at room temperature for about 1 hour until puffy, then bake.)

Preheat the oven to 400°F (200°C). Brush the rolls lightly with the egg wash. Bake until the rolls are golden brown and a toothpick inserted into the center of a roll comes out clean, about 25 minutes. Let the rolls cool slightly in the dish on a wire rack.

Meanwhile, make the icing: In a medium bowl, using an electric mixer, beat together the cream cheese and butter until very smooth. Beat in the vanilla. Sift the powdered sugar over the top and beat in on low speed. Gradually beat in enough of the milk to make a thick but spreadable icing. Using a metal icing spatula, spread the icing over the warm rolls. Let cool for 15 minutes. Serve warm or at room temperature.

SPICED APPLE CIDER MINI DOUGHNUT MUFFINS

MAKES ABOUT 40 MINI MUFFINS

FOR THE MUFFINS

1½ cups (185 g) all-purpose flour

½ cup (100 g) firmly packed dark brown sugar

1½ tsp baking powder

½ tsp baking soda

½ tsp kosher salt

1 tsp ground cinnamon

½ tsp pumpkin pie spice

½ cup (120 ml) apple cider syrup (see Note)

⅓ cup (80 ml) whole milk, at room temperature

2 large eggs, at room temperature

2 tbsp avocado oil or canola oil

2 tsp pure vanilla extract

FOR THE SPICED SUGAR TOPPING

½ cup (100 g) granulated sugar

½ tsp ground cinnamon

½ tsp pumpkin pie spice

4 tbsp (60 g) unsalted butter, melted

Cider doughnuts are a beloved autumn treat on the East Coast, and these easy-to-prepare muffins re-create those spicy flavors any time of the year, wherever you live. To amp up the cider taste, cook down apple cider into a syrup (see Note). The icing on the cake? Dipping the warm muffins into a sugar-and-spice mixture that adds both flavor and texture.

Preheat the oven to 350°F (180°C). Spray about 40 cups of two 24-cup mini muffin pans with cooking spray.

To make the muffins, in a bowl, whisk together the flour, brown sugar, baking powder, baking soda, salt, cinnamon, and pumpkin spice. In another bowl, whisk together the cider syrup, milk, eggs, oil, and vanilla. Pour the syrup mixture into the flour mixture and whisk until just combined.

Using a small cookie scoop, scoop the batter into the prepared muffin cups, filling each about three-fourths full.

Bake until the edges and tops are lightly browned, 8–10 minutes. Let cool for 2 minutes, then remove the muffins from the pan and transfer to a wire rack.

Meanwhile, make the spiced sugar topping. In a shallow bowl, stir together the granulated sugar, cinnamon and pumpkin pie spice. While still warm, dunk the top of each muffin into the melted butter, then press the tops into the sugar mixture. Serve right away.

NOTE: To make apple cider syrup, pour 1½ cups (350 ml) apple cider into a small saucepan and place over medium-low heat. Simmer until the cider reduces to ½ cup (120 ml), about 20 minutes. Let cool slightly before using.

CREAM-CURRANT SCONES WITH QUICK STRAWBERRY JAM

With their delicate texture and mildly sweet flavor, these buttery scones beg for a generous spoonful of fresh fruit jam—and there's nothing better than fresh strawberry jam. If you can find clotted cream, a dollop of it is a welcome, and traditional, addition to any scone spread. Serve a pot of tea alongside.

MAKES 8 SCONES

FOR THE QUICK STRAWBERRY JAM

1 lb (450 g) strawberries, stemmed, cored, and finely chopped

1 cup (200 g) sugar

2 tbsp fresh lemon juice

FOR THE SCONES

2 cups (250 g) all-purpose flour, plus more for dusting

3 tbsp sugar

2½ tsp baking powder

¼ tsp kosher salt

½ cup (115 g) cold unsalted butter, cut into pieces

½ cup (90 g) dried currants

1 cup (240 ml) heavy cream

Butter, clotted cream, or whipped cream for serving

To make the jam, place a saucer in the freezer to chill. Have ready a heatproof bowl set inside a larger bowl of ice water. In a saucepan, combine the strawberries, sugar, and lemon juice. Place over medium heat and bring to a boil, stirring constantly to dissolve the sugar. Reduce the heat to medium-low and cook, stirring occasionally, until the berries are very tender and the juices thicken, about 10 minutes. To test, remove the chilled saucer from the freezer, spoon about 1 tsp of the jam onto the saucer, and let stand for 15 seconds. If the liquid thickens to a jamlike consistency, then the jam is ready. If not, cook for 1–2 minutes longer. Transfer the jam to the bowl set in the bowl of ice water and let stand, stirring occasionally, until cooled and thickened.

To make the scones, preheat the oven to 400°F (200°C). Line a baking sheet with parchment paper.

In a bowl, sift together the flour, sugar, baking powder, and salt. Using a pastry blender or 2 knives, cut the butter into the flour mixture until the mixture looks like coarse bread crumbs. Stir in the currants. Pour the cream over the flour mixture and stir with a fork or rubber spatula just until combined.

Turn the dough out onto a lightly floured work surface. Using floured hands, pat out into a round about ½ inch (12 mm) thick. Using a 3-inch (7.5-cm) biscuit cutter, cut out as many rounds of the dough as possible. Gather up the scraps, knead briefly, and continue patting and cutting out to make 8 scones. Place 1 inch (2.5 cm) apart on the prepared baking sheet.

Bake until golden brown, 17–20 minutes. Transfer the scones to a wire rack and let cool slightly. Serve warm or at room temperature, with the strawberry jam and butter alongside.

RASPBERRY-LEMON STREUSEL MUFFINS

These light, cakey muffins contain bursts of fresh raspberries and tangy lemon zest, all topped with a crunchy sweet streusel. To change it up, swap out the raspberries for blueberries and add orange zest instead of lemon.

MAKES 16 MUFFINS

FOR THE STREUSEL

6 tbsp (90 g) unsalted butter, melted

1 tsp pure vanilla extract

1 cup (115 g) all-purpose flour

⅔ cup (140 g) sugar

¼ tsp kosher salt

FOR THE MUFFINS

2 cups (250 g) all-purpose flour

2 tsp baking powder

½ tsp baking soda

½ tsp kosher salt

4 tbsp (60 g) unsalted butter, at room temperature

¼ cup (60 ml) avocado oil or canola oil

⅔ cup (140 g) sugar

2 tsp grated lemon zest

2 large eggs

1 cup (450 g) sour cream

2 tbsp fresh lemon juice

1 cup (115 g) fresh or frozen raspberries

To make the streusel, in a medium bowl, stir together the melted butter and vanilla. In another bowl, combine the flour, sugar, and salt and stir together with a fork. Add the butter mixture and stir until evenly blended and crumbly. Set aside.

Preheat the oven to 400°F (200°C). Grease 16 standard muffin cups with cooking spray or line with paper liners.

To make the muffins, in a bowl, whisk together the flour, baking powder, baking soda, and salt. Set aside.

In a large bowl, using an electric mixer fitted with the paddle attachment, beat together the butter, oil, sugar, and lemon zest on medium-high speed until fluffy. Add the eggs and beat on medium-high speed until well blended. On low speed, beat in the sour cream and lemon juice, then add the flour mixture and beat on low speed until just moistened. Do not overmix. Fold in the raspberries with a rubber spatula.

Scoop the batter into the prepared muffin cups, filling each about three-fourths full (an ice cream scoop works well for this). Sprinkle with the streusel.

Bake until golden brown and a toothpick inserted into the center of a muffin comes out clean, about 17 minutes.

Transfer the pan to a wire rack and let cool for 15 minutes, then turn the muffins out onto the rack. Serve warm or at room temperature. Muffins can be stored in an airtight container at room temperature for up to 3 days.

LEMON–POPPY SEED DRIZZLE BREAD

MAKES ABOUT 8 SERVINGS

This extra-lemony bread boasts a triple dose of lemon flavor: lemon zest in the batter, lemon syrup for brushing on the warm bread after baking, and a lemon glaze for drizzling on the finished loaf. For a lemon-blueberry version, omit the poppy seeds and add 1 cup (140 g) fresh blueberries to the batter.

FOR THE BREAD
1½ cups (185 g) all-purpose flour

1 tsp baking powder

½ tsp kosher salt

½ cup (115 g) unsalted butter, at room temperature

¾ cup (140 g) granulated sugar

1 tbsp grated lemon zest

3 large eggs

½ cup (120 ml) whole milk

1 tsp pure vanilla extract

1 tbsp poppy seeds

FOR THE LEMON SYRUP
3 tbsp fresh lemon juice

3 tbsp granulated sugar

FOR THE LEMON GLAZE
½ cup (60 g) powdered sugar

3 tsp fresh lemon juice

Preheat the oven to 350°F (180°C). Butter and flour a 9-by-5-inch (23-by-13-cm) loaf pan.

To make the bread, in a bowl, sift together the flour, baking powder, and salt. Set aside.

Using an electric mixer fitted with the paddle attachment, beat together the butter, granulated sugar, and lemon zest on medium-high speed until well combined. Add the eggs, one at a time, beating until each is incorporated. Add the milk and vanilla and stir until blended. Add the flour mixture and the poppy seeds and stir just until blended.

Scrape the batter into the prepared pan. Bake until lightly browned and a toothpick inserted into the center comes out clean, about 50 minutes. Transfer the bread to a wire rack set over a rimmed baking sheet and let cool in the pan for a few minutes, then turn out onto the rack.

Meanwhile, make the syrup: In a small saucepan, combine the lemon juice and granulated sugar. Place over medium heat and bring to a boil, stirring until the sugar dissolves and the mixture becomes syrupy, about 2 minutes. Remove from the heat.

Using a wooden skewer, pierce the sides and bottom of the bread all over. While the bread is still warm, brush it generously with the syrup.

To make the glaze, in a small bowl, stir together the powdered sugar and lemon juice. When the bread is completely cool, drizzle the glaze over the top.

BUTTERMILK BISCUITS

MAKES 8 BISCUITS

2 cups (250 g) all-purpose flour

1 tbsp baking powder

½ tsp baking soda

1 tsp kosher salt

6 tbsp (90 g) cold unsalted butter, cut into ½-inch (12-mm) pieces

1 cup (250 ml) cold buttermilk

Lofty, flaky, and buttery, these biscuits are all that and more. The keys to great biscuits are keeping the ingredients cold, not overworking the dough, and eating them while they are still warm and fresh from the oven with plenty of butter (and honey if you like!).

Preheat the oven to 425°F (220°C). Line a rimmed baking sheet with parchment paper.

In a food processor, combine the flour, baking powder, baking soda, and salt and pulse a few times to mix. Add the butter and pulse 3 or 4 times, just until the mixture forms large, coarse crumbs the size of small peas. Pour in the buttermilk and pulse for a few seconds, until the flour mixture is moistened. Do not overmix.

Turn the dough out onto a lightly floured work surface and knead into a ball. Roll out into a round about ½ inch (12 mm) thick. Use a 3-inch (7.5-cm) biscuit cutter to cut out as many biscuits as you can. Gently gather up the scraps, knead into a ball, and roll out again. Repeat to cut out more biscuits; you should have 8 biscuits total. Place on the prepared baking sheet.

Bake until golden brown, about 15 minutes. Transfer the biscuits to a wire rack and let cool.

BREAKFAST FRUIT PUFFS

MAKES 4 PUFFS

All-purpose flour for dusting

1 sheet frozen puff pastry, thawed in the refrigerator but very cold

1 large egg beaten with 1 tsp water, for egg wash

Choice of toppings (pages 82–83)

Frozen puff pastry makes a quick and easy base for an endless combination of individual fruit tarts. For the best results, look for an all-butter puff pastry. After thawing it in the refrigerator, partially bake the puffs, then layer the pastry shells with fruit, brush with glaze, and continue baking to golden perfection.

Preheat the oven to 400°F (200°C). Line a baking sheet with parchment paper.

On a lightly floured work surface, gently roll out the puff pastry into a 9-inch (23-cm) square. Using a sharp paring knife, cut the pastry into 4 equal squares, then gently score a ¾-inch (2-cm) border around each square, carefully cutting halfway through the pastry. Using a fork, prick the center of each square to prevent puffing while baking.

Place the pastry squares well apart on the prepared baking sheet. Brush the entire surface of each square with the egg wash and bake for 7 minutes.

Remove the pan from the oven and add the topping(s) and glaze of your choice to the pastry shells as directed. Return the pan to the oven and bake until the pastries are golden brown and the fruit is tender, about 10 minutes longer.

Rhubarb-Strawberry Jam

Blackberry, Basil & Lemon Curd

Apple, Cinnamon-Sugar & Apple Jelly

Fresh Currant & Currant Jelly

Glazed Pear & Toasted Almond

Glazed Raspberry-Nutella

Blood Orange Marmalade

Glazed Apricot & Pistachio

Rhubarb–Strawberry Jam Fruit Puffs

6 tbsp (110 g) strawberry jam

1 stalk rhubarb, trimmed, cut crosswise into 3-inch (8-cm) pieces, then cut lengthwise into thin slices

1 tsp warm water

Spread 1 tbsp of the jam over the bottom of each pastry shell. Arrange the sliced rhubarb in a single layer on top. In a small bowl, stir together the remaining 2 tbsp jam and the warm water and brush over the rhubarb. Finish baking as directed.

Blackberry, Basil & Lemon Curd Fruit Puffs

4 tbsp (60 ml) homemade Lemon Curd (page 158) or store-bought

1 pint (250 g) blackberries

2 tbsp blackberry jam

1 tsp warm water

Fresh basil leaves for garnish (optional)

Spread 1 tbsp of the lemon curd over the bottom of each pastry shell. Arrange the blackberries in a single layer over the curd. In a small bowl, stir together the jam and warm water. Brush the jam mixture over the blackberries. Finish baking as directed. Sprinkle with basil leaves (if using) just before serving.

Glazed Pear & Toasted Almond Fruit Puffs

4 tbsp (70 g) pear jam or pear butter

3 tbsp cream cheese, at room temperature

2 firm but ripe pears, peeled, cored, and thinly sliced

1 tsp warm water

2 tbsp chopped toasted almonds (page 158)

In a small bowl, stir together 2 tbsp of the jam and the cream cheese. Spread 1 heaping tbsp of the jam-cheese mixture over the bottom of each pastry shell. Arrange the sliced pears, slightly overlapping, over the top. In another small bowl, stir together the remaining 2 tbsp jam and the warm water. Brush the jam mixture over the pears. Finish baking as directed. Sprinkle with the almonds just before serving.

Blood Orange Marmalade Fruit Puffs

6 tbsp (110 g) orange marmalade

2 blood oranges, peeled and cut into segments

1 tsp warm water

Spread 1 tbsp of the marmalade over the bottom of each pastry shell. Arrange the orange segments, slightly overlapping, over the marmalade. In a small bowl, stir together the remaining 2 tbsp marmalade and the warm water and brush over the oranges. Finish baking as directed.

Apple, Cinnamon-Sugar & Apple Jelly Fruit Puffs

6 tbsp (110 g) apple jelly

1 Granny Smith or other baking apple, cut crosswise into very thin slices

1 tsp warm water

Cinnamon sugar for sprinkling

Spread 1 tbsp of the jelly over the bottom of each pastry shell. Arrange 2 or 3 apple slices over the jelly on each tart. In a small bowl, stir together the remaining 2 tbsp jelly and the warm water and brush over the apples. Sprinkle with cinnamon sugar and finish baking as directed.

Glazed Raspberry-Nutella Fruit Puffs

4 tbsp (60 g) Nutella

1 cup (115 g) raspberries

2 tbsp raspberry jam

1 tsp warm water

Spread 1 tbsp of the Nutella over the bottom of each pastry shell. Arrange the raspberries in a single layer over the Nutella. In a small bowl, stir together the jam and warm water. Brush the jam mixture over the raspberries. Finish baking as directed.

Fresh Currant & Currant Jelly Fruit Puffs

8 tbsp (140 g) currant jelly

4–8 fresh currant sprigs

Powdered sugar for dusting

Spread 2 tbsp of the jelly over the bottom of each pastry shell. Finish baking as directed. Top each tart with fresh currant sprigs, then dust with powdered sugar.

Glazed Apricot & Pistachio Fruit Puffs

6 tbsp (110 g) apricot jam

6–8 fresh apricots, halved, pitted, and cut into thin wedges

1 tsp warm water

¼ cup (30 g) chopped raw pistachios

Spread 1 tbsp of the jam over the bottom of each pastry shell. Arrange the apricot wedges, slightly overlapping, on top. In a small bowl, stir together the remaining 2 tbsp jam and the warm water and brush over the apricots. Sprinkle the pistachios on top. Finish baking as directed.

SAVORY MUSHROOM & GOAT CHEESE TWISTS

MAKES 8 PASTRIES

1 tbsp olive oil

1 large shallot, finely chopped

8 oz (225 g) cremini mushrooms
or a mix of wild mushrooms, sliced

1 tsp minced fresh thyme

Kosher salt and freshly ground pepper

2 tbsp dry white wine

½ cup (70 g) crumbled goat or
feta cheese

All-purpose flour for dusting

2 sheets (450 g total) frozen
puff pastry, thawed in the refrigerator

1 egg beaten with 1 tsp water,
for egg wash

Featuring a classic Danish envelope shape, these savory puff pastries look like they took hours to make, but they couldn't be easier—especially with the use of frozen puff pastry. The filling combines cremini mushrooms, shallot, and goat cheese to create deliciously flavorful little tarts.

In a frying pan, warm the oil over medium heat. Add the shallot and cook, stirring, until softened, about 1 minute. Add the mushrooms and thyme and season with salt and pepper. Cook, stirring, until the mushrooms release their liquid and start to brown, about 5 minutes. Add the wine and cook just until evaporated. Let cool completely. Stir in the cheese.

Meanwhile, line 2 rimmed baking sheets with parchment paper. On a lightly floured surface, roll out each puff pastry sheet into a 9-inch (23-cm) square about ⅛ inch (3 mm) thick. Cut the square into four 4½-inch (11.5-cm) squares. You should have 8 squares.

Fold each square in half diagonally to create a triangle. Starting at the fold, cut a strip about 3½ inches (9 cm) long and about ¼ inch (6 mm) in from each edge, then repeat on the opposite side, keeping the area near the point of the triangle furthest from the fold intact. Unfold the square. Brush lightly with some of the egg wash. Gently pull 1 strip across the square to the opposite side, then repeat with the other strip, creating a frame. Brush the strips with egg wash.

Arrange 4 puff pastry squares on each prepared baking sheet. Refrigerate for at least 15 minutes or up to 2 hours.

Preheat the oven to 400°F (200°C).

Mound the mushroom filling onto the center of each puff pastry twist. Bake until golden brown and puffed, about 20 minutes. Serve warm.

HERB & OLIVE FOCACCIA

MAKES 8-10 SERVINGS

1 package (2¼ tsp) instant yeast

1¼ cups (300 ml) warm water (110°F/43°C)

3½–4 cups (425–500 g) bread flour, plus more for dusting

3½ tbsp olive oil, plus more for greasing

3 tbsp chopped fresh oregano, rosemary, and/or sage

1 tsp kosher salt

Freshly ground pepper

24 oil-cured black olives, pitted and chopped

Thick, fluffy slabs of focaccia make a terrific accompaniment to almost any egg dish, from scrambles, like the Caprese Scramble with Cherry Tomatoes, Basil & Mozzarella (page 25) to frittatas, such as the Roasted Red Pepper, Potato & Herb Frittata (page 31). If you don't like olives, simply omit them, and experiment with an array of chopped fresh or dried herbs.

In the bowl of a stand mixer, dissolve the yeast in the lukewarm water. Add 3 cups (425 g) of the flour, 2 tbsp of the oil, 1 tbsp of the herbs, the salt, and a few generous grinds of pepper. Fit the mixer with the dough hook, then knead on low speed until the ingredients come together. Raise the speed to medium and knead until the dough is soft and slightly sticky, 6–7 minutes, adding more flour as needed. Add flour as needed until the dough pulls away from the sides of the bowl.

Form the dough into a ball, transfer to a lightly oiled large bowl, turn to coat with the oil, and cover the bowl with plastic wrap. Let the dough rise in a warm, draft-free spot until it doubles in bulk, 45–60 minutes.

Meanwhile, in a small bowl, stir together the remaining 2 tbsp herbs, the olives, and 1 tbsp of the oil. Set aside.

Generously oil a rimmed baking sheet. Punch down the dough and turn out onto a lightly floured work surface. Form the dough into a ball, transfer to the prepared baking sheet, and let rest for 5 minutes. Using your fingers, stretch the dough so it evenly covers the bottom of the baking sheet. Cover the dough loosely with a kitchen towel and let rise in a warm, draft-free spot until puffy, 30–40 minutes.

Preheat the oven to 425°F (220°C).

Using your fingertips, make a pattern of dimples at 2-inch (5-cm) intervals over the entire surface of the dough. Brush with the remaining ½ tbsp oil and sprinkle with the olive mixture. Bake until golden brown, 18–20 minutes. Serve warm.

CHEDDAR-JALAPEÑO CORN BREAD

MAKES 6–8 SERVINGS

1¼ cups (140 g) fine yellow cornmeal

1 cup (115 g) all-purpose flour

2 tbsp sugar

2 tsp baking powder

1 tsp baking soda

½ tsp kosher salt

1¼ cups (300 ml) buttermilk

1 large egg

4 tbsp (60 g) unsalted butter, melted

¼ cup (35 g) drained and chopped pickled jalapeños

6 oz (170 g) sharp Cheddar cheese, grated

The addition of chopped pickled jalapeños and plenty of sharp Cheddar give this extra-savory corn bread a lot of pizzazz. For a simplified version—one that you can spread with butter and honey— just omit the jalapeños and cheese. Or stir ½ cup (90 g) fresh or frozen corn kernels into the batter to lend a pop of sweetness.

Preheat the oven to 375°F (190°C). Grease a 9-inch (23-cm) square baking pan with cooking spray.

In a medium bowl, whisk together the cornmeal, flour, sugar, baking powder, baking soda, and salt. Set aside.

In a large bowl, whisk together the buttermilk, egg, and melted butter until blended. Add the flour mixture and stir just until evenly moistened. Stir in the jalapeños and half of the cheese.

Pour the batter into the prepared pan and smooth the top. Sprinkle with the remaining cheese.

Bake until the top is golden brown and a toothpick inserted into the center comes out clean, about 16 minutes. Transfer to a wire rack and let cool in the pan for 5 minutes. Serve warm.

FRUITS & GRAINS

Oven-Roasted Fruit with Ricotta Cream 90

Fruit Smoothies 92

Green Smoothie Bowl 92

Chile-Lime Spiced Tropical Fruit Salad 93

Homemade Granola 95

Granola Parfaits with Fresh Fruit & Yogurt 98

Overnight Oats with Cacao Nibs & Raspberry Compote 99

Steel-Cut Oats with Honey-Glazed Pears & Pecans 101

Herbed Quinoa Breakfast Bowls with Avocado & Soft-Boiled Eggs 102

Chia Pudding with Fruit Compote 105

OVEN-ROASTED FRUIT WITH RICOTTA CREAM

MAKES 6–8 SERVINGS

1 cup (225 g) whole-milk ricotta cheese

¼ cup (60 g) crème fraîche

½ tsp pure vanilla extract

6 tbsp (90 g) sugar

2 peaches

2 nectarines

3 plums

8 fresh figs

½ lb (225 g) cherries, pitted

1 tbsp olive oil

Honey for serving

Roasting a medley of summer stone fruits deepens and caramelizes their flavors. A mixture of vanilla-scented, sweetened ricotta and crème fraîche adds a creamy and cooling complement to the rich fruit.

Preheat the oven to 475°F (245°C).

In a bowl, combine the ricotta, crème fraîche, vanilla, and 2 tbsp of the sugar and mix well. Cover and refrigerate until ready to use.

Halve the peaches, nectarines, and plums and remove the pits. Cut the halves in half again. Trim off the hard tip of each fig stem and leave the figs whole.

Combine all the fruits in a roasting pan or on a large rimmed baking sheet big enough to hold them in a single layer, drizzle with the oil, and turn to coat. Sprinkle with the remaining 4 tbsp (60 g) sugar and turn once or twice. Spread the fruit in an even layer.

Roast until the fruits are slightly collapsed and golden or lightly charred, 15–20 minutes.

Spoon the fruits and their cooking juices into bowls. Halve or quarter the figs lengthwise, if desired. Swirl a little honey into the ricotta mixture and serve with the fruit.

FRUIT SMOOTHIES

MAKES 2–4 SERVINGS

2 ripe bananas, peeled, frozen, and chopped

3 cups (425 g) chopped frozen fruit, such as pineapple, peach, mango, raspberries, blueberries, or strawberries

½ cup (130 g) vanilla yogurt

1½ cups (350 ml) fresh orange juice

Choose your own adventure by blending your favorite fruits with frozen banana, yogurt, and orange juice. Mixed berries, raspberry and peach, or mango and pineapple are all excellent combinations.

In a blender, combine the bananas, frozen fruit, yogurt, and orange juice and blend until thick and creamy. Pour into glasses and serve.

GREEN SMOOTHIE BOWL

MAKES 2 SERVINGS

1 cup (250 g) plain Greek yogurt

½ avocado, pitted and peeled

2 cups (60 g) spinach leaves

2 ripe bananas, peeled, frozen, and chopped

2 tbsp almond butter

1 mango, peeled, seeded, and sliced

1 cup (140 g) blueberries

1 tbsp toasted pepitas

1 tbsp toasted oat bran

Like a bowlful of delicious art, smoothie bowls are all about customizing and accessorizing. They are most appealing when topped with plenty of colorful fresh fruit and something crunchy— grains, nuts, and/or seeds—for texture. Use the toppings suggested here or experiment with whatever ingredients you like.

In a blender, combine the yogurt, avocado, spinach, bananas, and almond butter and blend until smooth. Spoon the smoothie into shallow bowls. Arrange the mango and blueberries on top. Sprinkle with the pepitas and oat bran, then serve.

CHILE-LIME SPICED TROPICAL FRUIT SALAD

MAKES 4–6 SERVINGS

3 cups (450 g) cubed seedless watermelon

2 cups (310 g) peeled, seeded, and cubed ripe mango

2 cups (310 g) pineapple chunks

2 cups (310 g) peeled, seeded, and cubed ripe papaya

2 limes

Chile-lime seasoning, preferably Tajín, to taste

Colorful cups of watermelon, mango, papaya, and/or jicama, cut into cubes or spears and sprinkled with lime and chili powder, are a popular Mexican street food. That balance of sweet tang and heat is captured in this bright and flavor-filled tropical fruit salad.

In a large bowl, toss together the watermelon, mango, pineapple, and papaya. Squeeze the juice of the limes over the fruit and toss to combine. Season with the chile-lime seasoning to taste. Serve at once, or cover and refrigerate for up to 4 hours before serving.

HOMEMADE GRANOLA

**MAKES ABOUT
3½ CUPS (400 G)**

The beauty of homemade granola is the infinite combinations you can create, limited only by your imagination (and likes and dislikes, of course). The basic method is simple: Mix oats and nuts, seeds, and/or spices, stir in warm sweetened oil, and bake in a low oven until crisp. Toss in any dried fruits or chocolate after baking. Store granola in an airtight container at room temperature for up to 2 weeks or in the freezer for up to 1 month.

Cinnamon-Almond Granola with Dried Blueberries

Nonstick cooking spray

2 cups (200 g) rolled oats

½ cup (70 g) chopped raw almonds

1 tsp ground cinnamon

¼ cup (60 ml) coconut oil

¼ cup (70 g) creamy peanut butter

¼ cup (80 g) pure maple syrup

½ tsp kosher salt

⅓ cup (40 g) dried blueberries

Preheat the oven to 300°F (150°C). Grease a baking sheet with cooking spray.

In a bowl, stir together the oats, almonds, and cinnamon; set aside. In a saucepan, combine the coconut oil, peanut butter, maple syrup, and salt. Place over medium heat and cook, stirring often, until smooth, 2–3 minutes. Pour over the oat mixture and stir to combine. Spread the mixture out on the prepared baking sheet.

Bake, stirring twice and rotating the pan once, until the granola is golden, about 25 minutes. Let cool completely on the baking sheet, then stir in the dried blueberries.

Maple-Pecan Granola with Toasted Coconut & Cranberries

Nonstick cooking spray

2 cups (200 g) rolled oats

½ cup (60 g) chopped pecans

½ cup (170 g) pure maple syrup

¼ cup (60 ml) coconut oil

1½ tsp pure vanilla extract

1 tsp ground cinnamon

¼ tsp kosher salt

½ cup (60 g) dried cranberries

⅓ cup (30 g) unsweetened flaked coconut, toasted (page 158)

Preheat the oven to 300°F (150°C). Grease a baking sheet with cooking spray.

In a large bowl, stir together the oats and pecans. Set aside. In a saucepan, combine the maple syrup, coconut oil, vanilla, cinnamon, and salt. Place over medium heat and cook, stirring occasionally, until smooth, 2–3 minutes. Pour over the oat mixture and stir to combine. Spread the mixture out on the prepared baking sheet.

Bake, stirring twice and rotating the pan once, until the granola is golden, about 25 minutes. Let cool completely on the baking sheet, then stir in the dried cranberries and coconut.

Granola with Roasted Peanuts, Dried Cherries & Chocolate

Nonstick cooking spray

2 cups (200 g) rolled oats

½ cup (60 g) roasted peanuts

½ cup (100 g) firmly packed light brown sugar

⅓ cup (60 g) honey

¼ cup (60 ml) coconut oil

1 tsp pure vanilla extract

1 tsp ground cinnamon

½ tsp kosher salt

½ cup (60 g) dried cherries

⅓ cup (60 g) semisweet chocolate chips

Preheat the oven to 300°F (150°C). Grease a baking sheet with cooking spray.

In a large bowl, stir together the oats and peanuts. Set aside. In a saucepan, combine the brown sugar, honey, coconut oil, vanilla, cinnamon, and salt. Place over medium heat and cook, stirring occasionally, until smooth, 2–3 minutes. Pour over the oat mixture and stir to combine. Spread the mixture out on the prepared baking sheet.

Bake, stirring twice and rotating the pan once, until the granola is golden, about 25 minutes. Let cool completely on the baking sheet, then stir in the dried cherries and chocolate chips.

Honey Granola with Dried Apricots & Pistachios

Nonstick cooking spray

2 cups (200 g) rolled oats

¾ cup (115 g) chopped raw pistachios

2 tbsp flaxseeds

½ cup (100 g) firmly packed light brown sugar

⅓ cup (60 g) honey

¼ cup (60 ml) coconut oil

2 tsp pure vanilla extract

1 tsp ground cinnamon

¼ tsp kosher salt

¾ cup (130 g) chopped dried apricots

Preheat the oven to 300°F (150°C). Grease a baking sheet with cooking spray.

In a large bowl, stir together the oats, pistachios, and flaxseeds. Set aside. In a saucepan, combine the brown sugar, honey, coconut oil, vanilla, cinnamon, and salt. Place over medium heat and cook, stirring occasionally, until smooth, 2–3 minutes. Pour over the oat mixture and stir to combine. Spread the mixture out on the prepared baking sheet.

Bake, stirring twice and rotating the pan once, until the granola is golden, about 25 minutes. Let cool completely on the baking sheet, then stir in the dried apricots.

GRANOLA PARFAITS WITH FRESH FRUIT & YOGURT

MAKES 4 SERVINGS

1½ cups (170 g) homemade granola
(pages 95–96) or store-bought

2 cups (500 g) vanilla yogurt

2 cups (285 g) mixed diced fresh fruit,
such as peaches, apricots, cherries,
raspberries, and/or blueberries

*What better way to serve your homemade granola (pages 95–96)
than in a pretty layered parfait with fresh fruit and your favorite
yogurt. If you assemble them in sturdy, unbreakable containers with
lids, they make the perfect breakfast on the go, and can be prepared
in advance and refrigerated.*

Set aside ¼ cup (28 g) of the granola. Divide half of the remaining granola
among 1-cup (240-ml) parfait glasses or tumblers. Top with half of the
yogurt and then half of the fruit, dividing evenly. Repeat the layers with
the remaining ingredients, ending with the fruit. Sprinkle the tops with the
reserved granola mixture. Refrigerate the parfaits for about 20 minutes,
then serve.

OVERNIGHT OATS WITH CACAO NIBS & RASPBERRY COMPOTE

MAKES 4 SERVINGS

FOR THE RASPBERRY COMPOTE

6 oz (170 g) raspberries

1–2 tbsp sugar

1 tsp fresh lemon juice

2 cups (200 g) rolled oats

2 cups (475 ml) whole milk or plant-based milk

1 cup (250 g) vanilla yogurt, plain yogurt, or plant-based yogurt

¼ cup (90 g) honey or pure maple syrup

4 tsp chia seeds (optional)

1 tsp pure vanilla extract

Kosher salt

1 cup (115 g) raspberries

¼ cup (30 g) cacao nibs

Overnight oats are the ultimate breakfast on the run. Not only is the dish incredibly versatile and delicious, but it's also made in advance and bonus: it's really good for you! Chia seeds give the oatmeal thick and creamy texture, and are full of amazing health benefits, including omega-3 fatty acids.

To make the compote, in a saucepan, stir together the raspberries, sugar, and lemon juice. Place over medium heat and bring to a simmer. Cook, stirring occasionally, until most of the berries have broken down and the mixture is thickened, about 15 minutes; reduce the heat if the compote sticks to the pan. Let the compote cool to room temperature, then transfer to an airtight container and refrigerate until chilled, about 2 hours or for up to 1 week.

Divide the oats, milk, yogurt, honey, chia seeds (if using), and vanilla among jars or tumblers. Add a pinch of salt to each and stir to combine. Cover the jars and refrigerate for at least 2 hours or up to overnight.

When ready to serve, top the oats with the fresh raspberries. Drizzle with the compote, garnish with the cacao nibs, and serve.

STEEL-CUT OATS WITH HONEY-GLAZED PEARS & PECANS

MAKES 4 SERVINGS

4 cups (950 ml) water

¼ tsp kosher salt

1 cup (200 g) steel-cut oats

1 tsp plus 1 tbsp unsalted butter

½ cup (60 g) pecans

2 tsp sugar

2 firm but ripe pears, such as Comice or Anjou, peeled, cored, and sliced or cut into chunks

3 tbsp honey

¼ tsp ground cinnamon

Half-and-half, heavy cream, or whole milk for serving

Healthy and hearty, oatmeal is a satisfying breakfast option that will start your day off right. Steel-cut oats take a little longer to cook but you are rewarded with their wonderful texture. Dress oatmeal up any way you like, but we particularly love this topping of caramelized pecans and sauteed pears with honey and cinnamon.

In a heavy saucepan, bring the water and salt to a boil over high heat. Stir in the oats and return to a boil. Reduce the heat to medium-low and simmer, stirring frequently to avoid scorching, until the oats are done to your preferred texture, 25–35 minutes.

Meanwhile, in a frying pan, melt 1 tsp of the butter over medium heat. Add the pecans and sprinkle with the sugar. Cook, stirring constantly, until the sugar melts and the pecans are toasted and glazed, about 1 minute. Transfer to a cutting board. Let the pecans cool slightly, then coarsely chop.

Rinse out and dry the frying pan. Just before the oatmeal is done, in the same pan, melt the remaining 1 tbsp butter over medium heat. Add the pears and cook, stirring occasionally, until they release some juices and are heated through, about 3 minutes. Add the honey and cinnamon and stir until the honey just melts.

Spoon the oats into bowls. Top with the pears and their juices and the pecans. Drizzle with half-and-half and serve.

HERBED QUINOA BREAKFAST BOWLS WITH AVOCADO & SOFT-BOILED EGGS

MAKES 4 SERVINGS

1 cup (170 g) quinoa

1 tsp kosher salt, plus more as needed

2 cups (475 ml) water

4 large eggs

1 small green onion, finely chopped

2 tbsp finely chopped fresh cilantro

2 tbsp finely chopped fresh mint

Dijon Vinaigrette (page 157)

Freshly ground pepper

4 cups (270 g) chopped baby kale, arugula, and/or mixed greens

1 avocado, pitted, peeled, and thinly sliced

Toasted pepitas for garnish, optional (page 158)

Packed with protein from the quinoa and egg and topped with vitamin-rich greens, herbs, and avocado, this savory power breakfast has it all. Feel free to experiment with grains like farro or brown rice, or try other seasonal vegetable combinations, like asparagus and sautéed mushrooms.

In a saucepan, combine the quinoa, salt, and water. Place over medium-high heat and bring to a boil. Cover, reduce the heat to low, and simmer until the water is absorbed, about 15 minutes. Fluff the quinoa and set aside until cooled.

Bring a large saucepan of water to a boil over medium-high heat. Gently lower the eggs into the water and cook for exactly 7 minutes for soft-boiled eggs. Drain the eggs and cool under running cold water for 30 seconds. Peel and halve the eggs.

In a bowl, stir together the quinoa, green onions, cilantro, and mint. Drizzle with a little vinaigrette, season with salt and pepper, and toss to combine.

Divide the kale among bowls and drizzle with a little vinaigrette. Top each salad with one-fourth of the quinoa mixture. Top each with one-fourth of the avocado and a halved egg. Season the avocado and egg with salt and pepper. Drizzle with vinaigrette. Garnish with pepitas (if using). Serve at once, passing any remaining vinaigrette alongside.

CHIA PUDDING WITH FRUIT COMPOTE

Loaded with fiber, protein, and omega-3 fatty acids, chia seeds are one of the most nutritious ingredients you can eat. They make a great choice for breakfast. Plumped in liquid overnight, the pudding is ready the next morning to be topped with your favorite combination of fresh fruit.

MAKES 4 SERVINGS

1 cup (240 ml) plant-based milk

¼ cup (40 g) chia seeds

2 tbsp pure maple syrup

1 tsp pure vanilla extract

1 cup (150 g) blackberries

2 kiwifruits, peeled and sliced

4 ripe apricots, pitted and cut into wedges

½ cup (75 g) pomegranate seeds or raspberries

¼ cup (20 g) coconut chips, toasted (page 158)

In a covered container, stir together the milk, chia seeds, maple syrup, and vanilla. Cover and refrigerate for at least 4 hours or up to overnight.

When ready to serve, stir the chia mixture and let stand at room temperature until the seeds are plumped, about 10 minutes. Divide the mixture among bowls and arrange the blackberries, kiwi, apricots, and pomegranate seeds on top. Sprinkle with the coconut chips and serve.

SALADS, TOASTS & SAVORIES

Mini Breakfast Pizzas with Eggs, Bacon & Parmesan 108

Smoked Salmon Salad with Tarragon Vinaigrette 110

Chicken, Spinach & Avocado Breakfast Quesadillas 111

New Orleans–Style Barbecue Shrimp & Grits 113

Grilled Shrimp Tacos with Pineapple Salsa 114

Chicken Hash with Bell Peppers & Herbs 115

Breakfast Salad with Soft-Boiled Eggs, Avocado & Bacon 116

Little Gems with Garlicky Bread Crumbs & Blue Cheese 117

Cannellini Bean, Tuna & Grilled Radicchio Salad 118

Curried Chicken Salad 120

Niçoise Salad 121

Savory Toasts 124

English Pea & Ricotta Tart 127

Grilled Eggplant, Red Pepper & Herbed Goat Cheese Sandwiches 128

Smoked Ham, Cheddar Cheese & Pear Panini 129

Loaded Bagel Bar 130

MINI BREAKFAST PIZZAS WITH EGGS, BACON & PARMESAN

MAKES 4 SERVINGS

Olive oil for greasing and brushing

All-purpose flour for dusting

1 lb (450 g) store-bought pizza dough, at room temperature

8 large slices thick-cut applewood-smoked bacon

½ cup (60 g) grated Parmesan cheese

4 large eggs

Kosher salt and freshly ground pepper

Chopped fresh chives for garnish

These playful breakfast pizzas will be a hit with the entire family, and when you use purchased pizza dough, they couldn't be easier. Partially bake the crusts and fry the bacon ahead of time, then when everyone is ready to eat, pop the pizzas in the oven to cook the eggs and breakfast is served!

Preheat the oven to 400°F (200°C). Oil a large rimless baking sheet.

On a lightly floured work surface, divide the dough into 4 equal pieces. Roll out each piece, stretching the dough if necessary, into a round 6–8 inches (15–20 cm) in diameter. Carefully transfer the rounds to the prepared baking sheet. The dough is elastic and will tend to lose shape; use oiled fingertips to reform the rounds on the pan, stretching and pulling the dough as needed. Brush with oil. Bake until puffed and lightly browned, about 10 minutes. Remove from the oven.

Meanwhile, in a large frying pan, cook the bacon over medium heat, turning a few times, until crisp and brown, about 8 minutes. Transfer to paper towels to drain. Cut the bacon into bite-size pieces and set aside.

Sprinkle one-fourth of the bacon and cheese over the top of each pizza. To prevent the egg yolks from breaking, crack each egg into a shallow bowl or saucer, then slide it onto the center of a pizza. Season lightly with salt and pepper.

Bake until the egg whites are set and the yolks are glazed over but still soft, about 10 minutes. Slide each pizza onto an individual plate, garnish with chives, and serve at once.

SMOKED SALMON SALAD WITH TARRAGON VINAIGRETTE

MAKES 4 SERVINGS

3 tbsp olive oil

2 tbsp white wine vinegar

3 tsp minced fresh tarragon

Kosher salt and freshly ground pepper

2 large bunches watercress,
tough stems removed, or 4 cups
(115 g) mâche lettuce

2 cups (60 g) baby arugula

1 small crisp-tart apple, such as
Honeycrisp, cored and thinly sliced

½ lb (225 g) hot-smoked salmon
or trout, skin and bones removed,
flaked with a fork

2½ tbsp snipped fresh chives

This main dish salad is a meal in a bowl or could be featured as part of a big brunch spread. It offers an excellent balance of peppery greens, smoky salmon, sweet-tart apple, and zesty tarragon vinaigrette. Pour a glass of your favorite sparkling wine to complete the meal.

In a large, wide serving bowl, whisk together the olive oil, vinegar, and tarragon. Season with salt and pepper.

Add the watercress, arugula, apple slices, and salmon and toss to coat with the vinaigrette.

Divide the salad among bowls or plates. Garnish with the chives and serve.

CHICKEN, SPINACH & AVOCADO BREAKFAST QUESADILLAS

MAKES 2 SERVINGS

4 large eggs

2 tbsp whole milk

¼ tsp kosher salt

⅛ tsp freshly ground pepper

1 tbsp olive oil

½ cup (90 g) shredded cooked chicken

1 cup (60 g) coarsely chopped baby spinach

½ cup (90 g) seeded and chopped tomatoes

2 large flour tortillas, each about 10 inches (25 cm) in diameter

⅔ cup (70 g) shredded sharp Cheddar cheese

¼ cup (60 g) sour cream

1 avocado, pitted, peeled, and sliced

¼ cup (60 ml) Pico de Gallo (page 157) or your favorite salsa

Stuffed with scrambled eggs, shredded chicken, fresh spinach, and sharp Cheddar cheese, these breakfast quesadillas are a hearty start to the day. For a vegetarian version, omit the chicken and add sautéed cremini mushrooms if you like.

Preheat the oven to 200°F (95°C).

In a bowl, whisk together the eggs, milk, salt, and pepper. In a frying pan, preferably nonstick, warm the oil over medium heat. Add the egg mixture and cook until the edges begin to set, about 20 seconds. Stir with a heatproof spatula, scraping up the eggs on the bottom and sides of the pan and folding them toward the center. Add the chicken, spinach, and tomatoes and continue cooking, stirring frequently, until the eggs are barely cooked into moist curds, about 1 minute. Remove the pan from the heat and set aside.

Heat another frying pan over medium heat. Place 1 tortilla in the pan and heat until warmed, about 1 minute. Flip the tortilla and sprinkle the bottom half with ⅓ cup (25 g) of the cheese. Top the cheese with half of the egg mixture. Fold the tortilla in half in the frying pan to cover the cheese and egg mixture. Continue cooking until the underside begins to brown, about 1 minute. Flip and cook the other side until it begins to brown, about 1 minute longer. Transfer to a baking sheet and keep warm in the oven. Repeat to make the second quesadilla.

Cut each quesadilla into wedges and divide between individual plates. Top each serving with half each of the sour cream, avocado, and pico de gallo. Serve at once.

NEW ORLEANS–STYLE BARBECUE SHRIMP & GRITS

MAKES 4 SERVINGS

FOR THE GRITS

1⅓ cups (200 g) stone-ground white corn grits

4 cups (950 ml) water

1⅓ cups (325 ml) whole milk

2 tsp kosher salt

6 tbsp (90 g) unsalted butter, cut into 6 pieces

FOR THE BARBECUE SHRIMP

1½ lb (680 g) medium shrimp, peeled and deveined

1 cup (240 ml) dark beer

¼ cup (60 ml) Worcestershire sauce

2 tbsp hot pepper sauce

1 tbsp fresh lemon juice

1 tsp minced fresh rosemary

1 tbsp cold unsalted butter

The name of this savory Southern classic is a bit confusing— there's no grilling involved and there's no barbecue sauce! A staple breakfast and brunch dish in New Orleans, the shrimp are cooked in a buttery beer-spiked sauce, then served over creamy stone-ground grits for a simple but delicious, meal.

To make the grits, place the grits in a large bowl and add enough cold water to cover by 1 inch (2.5 cm). Let stand for 5 minutes. Skim off any bran or hulls floating on the surface. Drain the grits in a fine-mesh sieve.

Meanwhile, in a large, heavy saucepan, bring the water, milk, and salt to a boil over high heat. Gradually whisk in the grits. Reduce the heat to low and simmer, whisking every 5 minutes, until the grits are thick and tender, about 45 minutes. Remove from the heat and whisk in the butter, 1 tbsp at a time.

To make the shrimp, about 10 minutes before the grits are done, heat a large frying pan over medium-high heat. Add the shrimp and cook until seared on one side, about 1 minute. Transfer to a bowl.

Add the beer, Worcestershire sauce, hot pepper sauce, and lemon juice to the pan and stir to scrape up the browned bits on the bottom of the pan. Cook, stirring frequently, until reduced by about one-third, about 5 minutes. Return the shrimp to the pan and cook until opaque throughout, about 1 minute. Remove from the heat and stir in the rosemary. Add the butter and stir until melted and the sauce is lightly thickened (the sauce will still be thin).

Spoon the grits into bowls. Top with the shrimp and sauce, then serve.

GRILLED SHRIMP TACOS WITH PINEAPPLE SALSA

MAKES 4 SERVINGS

FOR THE PINEAPPLE SALSA

2 cups (340 g) diced fresh pineapple

½ small red onion, finely chopped

½ small red bell pepper, seeded and finely chopped

1 small cucumber, peeled and diced

½ jalapeño chile, seeded and finely chopped

½ cup (30 g) chopped fresh cilantro

2 tbsp fresh lime juice

2 tbsp olive oil

Kosher salt and freshly ground pepper

FOR THE SHRIMP TACOS

Olive oil for brushing

24 medium shrimp, about 1 lb (450 g) total, peeled and deveined

4 tbsp (60 g) unsalted butter

½ tsp chipotle chile powder

1 small clove garlic, minced

8 corn tortillas, each about 6 inches (15 cm) in diameter

Fresh, tangy, and spicy-sweet, this pineapple salsa is the perfect topping for grilled, chile-rubbed shrimp. Tuck the shrimp and salsa into corn tortillas for tacos, or serve them atop a bed of greens for a gorgeous brunch salad.

To make the salsa, in a large bowl, combine the pineapple, onion, bell pepper, cucumber, jalapeño, and cilantro. Add the lime juice and olive oil, then season with salt and pepper. Stir well to combine. Cover and refrigerate until ready to serve.

To make the tacos, prepare a charcoal or gas grill for direct grilling over medium-high heat. Oil the rack.

Thread the shrimp on long metal skewers. In a small saucepan, melt the butter over medium-high heat. Remove from the heat, let cool slightly, and stir in the chile powder and garlic. Brush the shrimp with some of the butter mixture.

Using tongs, place the shrimp over the hottest part of the fire or directly over the heat elements and grill until bright pink, about 2 minutes. Turn and grill until bright pink on the second side, about 2 minutes longer. The shrimp should be firm to the touch at the thickest part. Transfer to a plate.

Lightly brush the tortillas with the remaining butter mixture and place over the hottest part of the grill. Grill until they start to puff up, about 1 minute. Using tongs, turn and grill until puffed on the second sides, about 1 minute longer.

Place 2 tortillas on each plate. Arrange 3 shrimp in the center of each tortilla and top with a spoonful of the salsa. Serve at once, passing the remaining salsa at the table.

CHICKEN HASH WITH BELL PEPPERS & HERBS

MAKES 6 SERVINGS

1¾ lb (800 g) skin-on, bone-in chicken breast halves

2 cups (475 ml) low-sodium chicken stock

1 small yellow onion, sliced

½ tsp kosher salt, plus more as needed

¼ tsp freshly ground pepper, plus more as needed

1½ lb (680 g) small russet potatoes, peeled and quartered

7 tbsp (100 g) unsalted butter

1 small red bell pepper, seeded and chopped

1 small orange or yellow bell pepper, seeded and chopped

3 tbsp minced shallots

3 tbsp all-purpose flour

2 tbsp heavy cream

2 tsp minced fresh rosemary

2 tsp minced fresh sage

Chopped fresh chives for garnish

Flavored boldly with shallots, rosemary, and sage, this succulent chicken hash is an ideal marriage of peppers, potatoes, and onions. To save time, use 2 cups (340 g) chopped leftover chicken and 1½ cups (350 ml) premade chicken stock. A heavy frying pan and a gentle press with a spatula while cooking will guarantee a crisp, golden crust.

In a large saucepan, combine the chicken breasts, broth, onion, salt, and pepper. Add enough cold water to barely cover the chicken. Bring to a boil over high heat, then reduce the heat to low and simmer gently until the chicken shows no sign of pink when pierced with a sharp knife, about 30 minutes. Transfer to a cutting board and let stand until cool enough to handle.

Strain the stock through a fine-mesh sieve and measure 1½ cups (350 ml); set aside. Reserve the remaining stock for another use; discard the onion. Remove and discard the skin and bones from the chicken. Cube the meat and transfer to a large bowl.

Meanwhile, put the potatoes in another saucepan and add enough salted water to cover. Bring to a boil over high heat. Reduce the heat to medium-low, cover, and simmer until the potatoes are tender when pierced with the tip of a sharp knife, about 20 minutes. Drain and rinse under cold running water. Let the potatoes stand until cool enough to handle, then cube. Add to the chicken.

In a large frying pan, preferably nonstick, melt 2 tbsp of the butter over medium heat. Add the bell peppers and cook, stirring frequently, until tender, about 5 minutes. Add the shallots and cook, stirring occasionally, until tender, about 2 minutes. Add to the chicken and potatoes.

In a saucepan, melt 3 tbsp of the butter over medium-low heat. Whisk in the flour and let bubble for 1 minute without browning. Gradually whisk in the 1½ cups (350 ml) reserved stock, raise the heat to medium, and bring to a boil, whisking frequently. Reduce the heat to medium-low and cook, whisking frequently, until reduced by about one-third, 8–10 minutes. Stir in the cream. Add to the chicken mixture along with the rosemary and sage, and stir well, breaking up the potatoes with the side of the spoon. Season with salt and pepper.

Wipe out the frying pan with paper towels. Add the remaining 2 tbsp butter to the pan and melt over medium-high heat. Add the chicken mixture, then press it into a flat disk with a metal spatula. Cook until browned and crispy, 4–5 minutes. Using the spatula, turn sections of the hash over (it should not remain whole) and press down again. Cook until the second side is browned, 4–5 minutes longer.

Divide the hash among individual bowls, sprinkle with chives, and serve at once.

BREAKFAST SALAD WITH SOFT-BOILED EGGS, AVOCADO & BACON

MAKES 4 SERVINGS

4–8 large eggs

8 large slices thick-cut applewood-smoked bacon

About 6 cups (210 g) mixed salad greens

Dijon Vinaigrette (page 157)

2 small avocados, pitted, peeled, and thinly sliced

Kosher salt and freshly ground pepper

½ cup (120 ml) of your favorite salsa

Salad for breakfast? Yes, please! With creamy boiled eggs, plenty of crisp bacon, creamy avocado, and a dollop of your favorite salsa, this salad is terrific any time of the day. Serve it with thick slices of buttered toast or homemade Buttermilk Biscuits (page 77).

Bring a large saucepan of water to a boil over medium-high heat. Gently lower the eggs into the water and cook for exactly 7 minutes for soft-boiled eggs. Drain the eggs and cool under running cold water for 30 seconds. Peel the eggs, cut in half, and set aside.

In a large frying pan, cook the bacon over medium heat, turning a few times, until crisp and brown, about 8 minutes. Transfer to paper towels to drain. Chop the bacon into bite-size pieces.

In a large bowl, toss the greens with some of the vinaigrette. Divide among shallow bowls or plates. Sprinkle the bacon over the greens. Top each salad with half an avocado, fanning out the slices, and 1–2 eggs. Season with salt and pepper. Top the salads with a dollop of salsa and serve, passing the remaining vinaigrette and salsa alongside.

LITTLE GEMS WITH GARLICKY BREAD CRUMBS & BLUE CHEESE

MAKES 4 SERVINGS

FOR THE GARLICKY BREAD CRUMBS

2 slices artisan-style bread, each about ½ inch (12 mm) thick

Olive oil for brushing

1 large clove garlic, peeled

FOR THE SALAD

¼ cup (60 ml) olive oil

2 oz (60 g) blue cheese, crumbled

1½ tbsp red wine vinegar

4 large heads little gem lettuce

¼ cup (15 g) minced fresh flat-leaf parsley

A cross between butter lettuce and romaine, little gems combine the best of both lettuces. Crunchy and tender with a mild taste, they are an excellent foundation for strong flavors and layers of texture. Here, crisp garlicky bread crumbs are sprinkled over blue cheese crumbles and fresh parsley for a salad that goes easily with just about any main dish.

Preheat the oven to 350°F (180°C).

To make the bread crumbs, brush both sides of each bread slice with oil. Place the bread slices on a baking sheet and bake, turning once, until crisp and dry, 15–18 minutes. Rub one side of each slice with the garlic clove. Let cool, then break the bread into chunks. Put in a food processor and process until coarse crumbs form. Transfer to a small bowl.

To make the salad, in a small bowl, combine the oil and cheese. Using a fork, mash the blue cheese into the oil to make a creamy dressing. Stir in the vinegar.

Cut each little gem lettuce head lengthwise into quarters. Place on a platter or on individual plates. Drizzle generously with the dressing. Sprinkle with the parsley and top with the garlicky bread crumbs. Serve at once.

CANNELLINI BEAN, TUNA & GRILLED RADICCHIO SALAD

MAKES 4-6 SERVINGS

FOR THE BEANS

1 cup (225 g) dried cannellini beans

2 tbsp olive oil

1–2 cloves garlic

1 fresh sage sprig

FOR THE SALAD

2 small heads radicchio

Kosher salt and freshly ground pepper

1 cup (140 g) chopped celery, including some leaves

½ small red onion, chopped

Pinch of dried oregano

2 tbsp olive oil, plus more for brushing

1–2 tbsp fresh lemon juice

1 can (220 g) olive oil–packed tuna, drained and separated into chunks

Radicchio is a stout, slightly bitter vegetable that holds up well to grilling–imparting a bit of smokiness while tenderizing it. Mixed with creamy cannellini beans, crunchy celery, and flaked canned tuna, this delightful salad can stand on its own as a main course.

To make the beans, rinse the beans, put them in a bowl. Add water to cover by about 3 inches (7.5 cm). Let soak for at least 4 hours or up to overnight.

Drain the beans. Place them in a saucepan and add water to cover. Bring to a boil over high heat, then add the oil, garlic, and sage. Cover, reduce the heat to low, and simmer gently until the beans are tender but not falling apart, about 1 hour. Remove from the heat and let stand for 10 minutes, then drain well and transfer to a bowl. Set aside to cool.

To make the salad, prepare a charcoal or gas grill for direct grilling over medium-high heat or preheat a broiler. Oil the grill rack.

Cut each radicchio head lengthwise into 4–6 wedges through the core, so that the wedges will keep their shape. Brush with oil and season with salt and pepper.

To grill the radicchio, using tongs, place the radicchio wedges over the hottest part of the fire or directly over the heat elements and grill, turning once, until wilted and lightly browned, about 5 minutes total. To broil the radicchio, arrange the radicchio wedges in a single layer on a rimmed baking sheet and place in the broiler. Broil, turning once, until wilted and lightly browned, about 5 minutes total.

Add the celery, onion, oregano, oil, and 1 tbsp of the lemon juice to the beans. Season with salt and pepper and toss well. Toss well. Taste and adjust the seasoning with more lemon juice, salt, and pepper as needed.

Arrange the radicchio wedges on a platter. Spoon the beans in the center and top with the tuna. Serve at once.

CURRIED CHICKEN SALAD

MAKES 4–6 SERVINGS

Curried chicken salad is a mainstay in many well-stocked delis—it makes a terrific sandwich filling or can be served atop a bed of lettuces. There are many versions, some that lean toward the sweeter side, studded with raisins or currants, and others—like this one—that are more savory, with plenty of fresh herbs and spices.

FOR THE CHICKEN

3 skin-on, bone-in chicken breast halves, about 1½ lb (680 g) total

Kosher salt and freshly ground pepper

1 tbsp olive oil

3 fresh rosemary sprigs, each 2 inches (5 cm) long

½ cup (120 ml) dry white wine, such as Sauvignon Blanc or Pinot Grigio

¼ cup (60 ml) water, plus more as needed

FOR THE SALAD

¼ cup (60 ml) mayonnaise

¼ cup (60 g) plain nonfat yogurt

3 tbsp crème fraîche

1 tsp ground cumin

½ tsp ground turmeric

½ tsp kosher salt

½ tsp freshly ground black pepper

¼ tsp cayenne pepper

3 celery stalks, finely chopped

4 green onions, white and green parts, thinly sliced

¼ cup (15 g) chopped fresh flat-leaf parsley, plus sprigs for garnish

¼ cup (30 g) chopped almonds or cashews (optional)

To make the chicken, season the chicken breasts all over with salt and pepper. In a large frying pan, warm the oil over medium-high heat. Add the chicken breasts, skin sides down, and cook until golden, about 5 minutes. Add the rosemary, turn the chicken breasts over, and cook until brown on the second sides, 4–5 minutes longer. Pour in the wine and stir, scraping up any browned bits from the pan bottom. Add the water, cover, reduce the heat to low, and cook, adding more water if needed, until the chicken is opaque throughout, about 35 minutes. Let cool. The chicken can be cooked ahead, covered, and refrigerated overnight.

Remove and discard the skin and bones from the chicken breasts. Cut the meat into ½-inch (12-mm) cubes. Set aside.

To make the salad, in a large bowl, whisk together the mayonnaise, yogurt, crème fraîche, cumin, turmeric, salt, black pepper, and cayenne. Add the cooked chicken, celery, green onions, parsley, and almonds (if using). Stir to coat with the mayonnaise mixture.

Transfer the salad to a serving bowl or platter and garnish with the parsley sprigs. Serve at once.

NIÇOISE SALAD

MAKES 6 SERVINGS

Kosher salt and freshly ground pepper

6 small waxy potatoes

1 lb (450 g) green beans, trimmed

1 large head butter lettuce,
leaves separated

6 small ripe heirloom tomatoes,
cut into wedges

1 small English cucumber, sliced

6 hard-boiled eggs, peeled and
quartered

2 cans (220 g each) olive oil–packed
tuna, drained and flaked

12 olive oil–packed anchovy fillets,
halved lengthwise (optional)

⅔ cup (90 g) Niçoise olives

12 fresh basil leaves, torn

½ cup (120 ml) olive oil

¼ cup (60 ml) red wine vinegar

This classic composed salad features peak-of-season summer produce: green beans, heirloom tomatoes, cucumbers, basil, and butter lettuce. Arrange the ingredients on a large platter to serve family-style, or divide everything among plates for individual servings.

Bring a saucepan three-fourths full of salted water to a boil over high heat. Add the potatoes and cook until tender, about 10 minutes. Drain, place under cold running water until cool, and drain again. Cut into slices ¼ inch (6 mm) thick. Set aside.

Refill the saucepan three-fourths full of salted water and bring to a boil. Add the green beans and cook until tender, 2–3 minutes. Drain, place under cold running water until cool, and drain again. Set aside.

Line individual plates with the lettuce leaves. Arrange the potatoes, green beans, tomatoes, cucumber, eggs, tuna, anchovies (if using), and olives on the lettuce. Garnish with the basil.

In a bowl, whisk together the oil and vinegar. Season with salt and pepper. Pour the vinaigrette over the salad. Serve at once.

Avocado Toasts with Watercress,
Sunflower Seeds & Flaky Sea Salt

Smoked Salmon Toasts with
Dill Cream, Red Onion & Capers

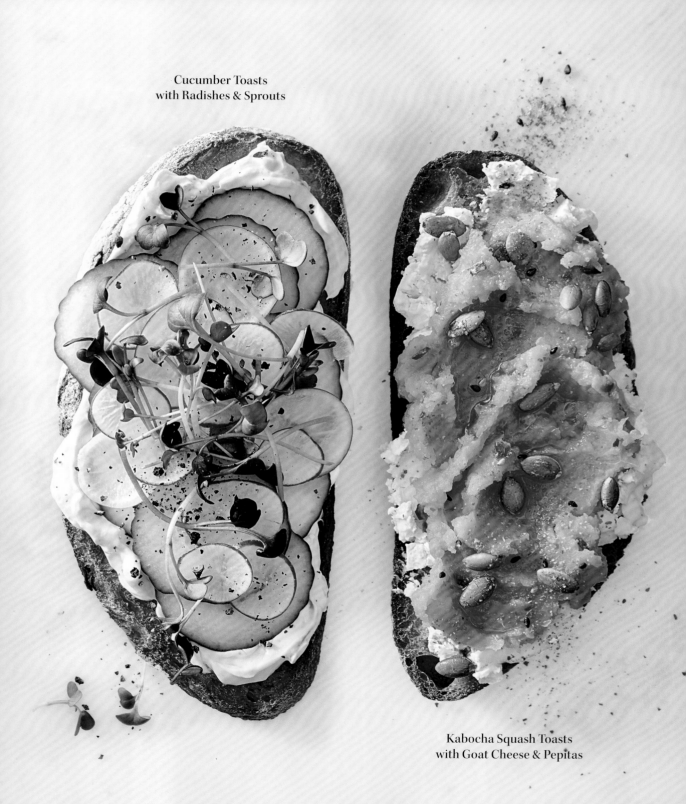

Cucumber Toasts
with Radishes & Sprouts

Kabocha Squash Toasts
with Goat Cheese & Pepitas

SAVORY TOASTS

Piled high with flavorful ingredients, these inspired toasts will keep you satisfied all day long. Use the best-quality bread you can, such as a crusty country loaf, levain, multi-grain, or even walnut bread.

MAKES 2–4 SERVINGS

Avocado Toasts with Watercress, Sunflower Seeds & Flaky Sea Salt

4 slices whole-grain bread, toasted

1½ avocados, pitted, peeled, and thinly sliced

1½ cups (40 g) watercress, tough stems removed

2 tbsp olive oil

4 tsp fresh lemon juice

2 tbsp roasted unsalted sunflower seeds

Flaky sea salt, such as Maldon

Top each toast with the avocado slices, slightly overlapping. In a small bowl, toss the watercress with the oil and lemon juice and pile high on top of the avocados. Sprinkle with the sunflower seeds and flaky sea salt, then serve.

Smoked Salmon Toasts with Dill Cream, Red Onion & Capers

6 oz (170 g) cream cheese, at room temperature

2 tbsp chopped fresh dill

1 tsp fresh lemon juice

Kosher salt and freshly ground pepper

4 slices whole-grain bread, toasted

¼ lb (115 g) thinly sliced smoked salmon

¼ cup (30 g) thinly sliced red onion

2 tbsp capers

1 tbsp finely chopped fresh chives

In a small bowl, stir together the cream cheese, dill, and lemon juice. Season to taste with salt and pepper. Spread the cream cheese mixture on the toasts. Top with the smoked salmon, onion, capers, and chives, then serve.

Kabocha Squash Toasts with Goat Cheese & Pepitas

½ kabocha squash, seeded, peeled, and cut into ½-inch (12-mm) pieces

3 tbsp olive oil

Kosher salt and freshly ground pepper

½ small yellow onion, finely chopped

1 tsp red pepper flakes

4 oz (115 g) goat cheese, at room temperature

4 slices whole-grain bread, toasted

2 tbsp toasted pepitas

Shichimi togarashi or chile oil for garnish

Preheat the oven to 450°F (230°C). Line a baking sheet with parchment paper. Place the squash on the prepared baking sheet, toss with 2 tbsp of the oil, and spread in a single layer. Season generously with salt and pepper. Roast, stirring once, until soft and caramelized, 25–30 minutes.

In a frying pan, warm the remaining 1 tbsp olive oil over medium-high heat. Add the onion and cook, stirring occasionally, until softened, about 5 minutes. Add the red pepper flakes and cook, stirring occasionally, for 1 minute. Add the squash and stir to combine. Using a potato masher or a large fork, mash the squash mixture.

Spread the goat cheese on the toasts. Top with the squash mixture and sprinkle with the pepitas. Sprinkle with shichimi togarashi or drizzle with chile oil, then serve.

Cucumber Toasts with Radishes & Sprouts

4 oz (115 g) cream cheese, at room temperature

2 oz (60 g) feta cheese, at room temperature

2 tbsp thinly sliced green onion, white and green parts

½ tsp minced garlic

Kosher salt and freshly ground pepper

4 slices whole-grain bread, toasted

½ English cucumber, thinly sliced

2 radishes, thinly sliced

¼ cup (10 g) alfalfa sprouts or other sprouts

In a small bowl, stir together the cream cheese, feta cheese, green onion, and garlic. Season to taste with salt and pepper. Spread the cream cheese mixture on the toasts. Top with the cucumber, radishes, and sprouts. Season with salt and pepper, then serve.

ENGLISH PEA & RICOTTA TART

MAKES 4–6 SERVINGS

One 8-by-10-inch (20-by-25-cm) sheet frozen puff pastry, thawed in the refrigerator

1⅓ cups (185 g) shelled peas

1 cup (225 g) whole-milk ricotta cheese, drained

3 tbsp finely chopped fresh mint, plus small leaves for garnish

1 tsp minced lemon zest

Kosher salt and freshly ground pepper

¼ cup (15 g) fresh flat-leaf parsley leaves

2 green onions, white and green parts, very thinly sliced on the diagonal

Fresh lemon juice to taste

Pea shoots for garnish (optional)

This delightful tart showcases the best of springtime produce. A delicate base of crisp puff pastry is spread with a pea and ricotta puree flavored with mint and lemon zest. Whole peas, pea shoots, mint, and green onions top the tart and give it another layer of texture. Sliced, blanched asparagus would be a great addition as well.

Preheat the oven to 400°F (200°C). Line a baking sheet with parchment paper. Place the puff pastry on the prepared baking sheet and bake until puffed, 10–13 minutes. Remove from the oven, top with a sheet of parchment paper and another baking sheet, and bake until golden and crisp, 10–13 minutes. Remove the top baking sheet and parchment paper and let the pastry cool.

Bring a pot of salted water to a boil over high heat. Add the peas and cook until tender, 2–3 minutes. Drain and rinse briefly under cold running water. Reserve ⅓ cup (40 g) of the peas. In a food processor, combine the remaining peas, the ricotta, and 1 tbsp of the chopped mint and process to make a chunky puree. Stir in the lemon zest and season with salt and pepper.

In a small bowl, stir together the parsley, the remaining 2 tbsp mint, the green onions, and the reserved peas. Season with salt and lemon juice.

Spread the ricotta mixture over the pastry and top with the parsley mixture. Garnish with mint leaves and pea shoots (if using). Cut into slices and serve.

GRILLED EGGPLANT, RED PEPPER & HERBED GOAT CHEESE SANDWICHES

MAKES 4 SERVINGS

2 tbsp red wine vinegar

2 tbsp olive oil, plus more for brushing

1 tsp chopped fresh thyme

1 tsp chopped fresh rosemary

1 clove garlic, minced

½ tsp kosher salt, plus more as needed

¼ tsp freshly ground pepper,
plus more as needed

½ large eggplant, about ¾ lb (340 g),
cut crosswise into slices ¼ inch
(6 mm) thick

1 red bell pepper

4 large ciabatta rolls or crusty
French rolls, split

4 oz (115 g) herbed fresh goat
cheese, softened

8–12 large fresh basil leaves

The eggplant and peppers benefit from the smoke and char of a charcoal or gas grill, but if you don't have time to fire it up, a searingly hot stovetop grill pan is a great alternative. For a perfect brunch picnic, tuck the ingredients into lightly crusty ciabatta rolls, wrap them up, and enjoy alfresco.

In a large bowl, whisk together the vinegar, oil, thyme, rosemary, garlic, salt, and pepper. Add the eggplant slices and turn to coat. Let marinate at room temperature for 1 hour.

Prepare a charcoal or gas grill for direct grilling over medium-high heat. Oil the grill rack.

Using tongs, place the bell pepper over the hottest part of the fire or directly over the heat elements and grill, turning as needed, until the skin is blistered and charred black on all sides, about 15 minutes. Transfer the pepper to a paper bag, close the bag, and let stand until cool enough to handle.

Remove the eggplant slices from the marinade. Grill, turning once, until softened, about 10 minutes total. Transfer to a plate and keep warm. Place the rolls, cut side down, on the grill until toasted, 1–2 minutes.

Remove the stem from the pepper and discard. Slit the pepper open, then cut away and discard the ribs and seeds. Remove the blackened skin with a small knife or your fingers. Cut lengthwise into ¼-inch (6-mm) strips.

Spread the bottom halves of the rolls with the goat cheese. Divide the eggplant slices among the rolls and top with the bell pepper strips. Season with salt and pepper. Lay 2 or 3 basil leaves on each sandwich. Cover with the top halves of the rolls. Cut each sandwich in half or into quarters. Arrange on individual plates and serve at once.

SMOKED HAM, CHEDDAR & PEAR PANINI

MAKES 4 SERVINGS

8 thick slices multigrain bread

½ cup (115 g) whole-grain mustard

½ lb (225 g) thinly sliced smoked ham

1 firm but ripe Bartlett pear, peeled, cored and cut into slices about ¼ inch (6 mm) thick

½ lb (225 g) Cheddar cheese, thinly sliced

Olive oil for brushing

This elevated grilled cheese sandwich includes salty-smoky ham and thin slices of ripe pear to add just a touch of sweetness. Thin apple slices or even a smear of fruit chutney can stand in for the pear. For a vegetarian version, simply leave out the ham.

Spread the bread slices on one side with the mustard. Divide the ham among 4 of the slices. Top with the pear slices and then with the cheese. Top with the remaining bread slices, mustard side down.

Heat a large grill pan or heavy frying pan over medium-high heat. Brush the outsides of the sandwiches with oil. When the pan is hot, place 2 sandwiches in the center. Set another heavy pan on top of the sandwiches and place 2 or 3 heavy cans in the pan to weight it down evenly. Cook the sandwiches until lightly browned on the first sides, about 3 minutes. Turn the sandwiches, weight them down again, and cook until browned on the second sides and the cheese is melting, about 3 minutes longer. Transfer the sandwiches to a cutting board and tent with aluminum foil to keep warm. Repeat to cook the remaining 2 sandwiches.

Cut the sandwiches in half, place on individual plates, and serve at once.

Prosciutto, Fresh Mozzarella & Basil

Sliced Tomatoes, Scrambled Eggs & Chives

**Sun-Dried Tomato Cream Cheese,
Carrot, Avocado & Olives**

**Blueberries, Cream Cheese,
Honey & Fresh Edible Blossoms**

Smoked Trout, Cream Cheese, Caper Berries & Red Onion

Cherry Tomatoes, Cambozola, Bacon & Arugula

LOADED BAGEL BAR

Setting up a brunchtime bagel bar with an array of flavored schmears and toppings— like sliced heirloom tomatoes, cucumbers, avocado, and smoked salmon—is a terrific way to entertain a crowd. For best results, purchase bagels the day you'll be serving them. To toast multiple bagels, split them in half horizontally and place them, cut side up, on a baking sheet, then broil until toasty and golden brown.

Nutella, Sliced Bananas, Pistachios & Toasted Coconut

DRINKS

Watermelon-Lime Agua Fresca 134

Sparkling Ginger Lemonade 134

Bellini Bar 138

Blood Orange Mimosa 139

Summer Fruit Rosé Sangria 139

Balsamic Bloody Mary 141

Michelada 141

Cold Brew Vanilla Bean Iced Coffee 142

Chai Latte 142

Spicy Hot Cocoa 143

WATERMELON-LIME AGUA FRESCA

MAKES 6–8 SERVINGS

½ cup (120 ml) plus 4 cups
(950 ml) water

½ cup (100 g) sugar

8 cups (1.1 kg) seedless
watermelon chunks

1 cup (240 ml) fresh lime juice

Ice cubes

Have ready a bowl of ice water. In a small saucepan over medium heat, combine ½ cup (120 ml) of the water with the sugar, stirring until the sugar is dissolved. Place the saucepan in the ice bath to cool the simple syrup quickly. Let cool completely.

In a blender, working in batches if necessary, combine the remaining 4 cups (950 ml) water with the watermelon, lime juice, and simple syrup. Blend until completely liquid and frothy. Strain through a fine-mesh sieve into a pitcher.

Fill glasses with ice cubes, pour in the watermelon agua fresca, and serve.

SPARKLING GINGER LEMONADE

MAKES 6 SERVINGS

4 cups (950 ml) water

¾ cup (140 g) sugar, or to taste

½ cup (60 g) peeled and thinly
sliced fresh ginger

¾ cup (180 ml) fresh lemon juice,
or to taste

2½ cups (600 ml) well-chilled
sparkling water, or to taste

Ice cubes

6 lemon slices for garnish

6 strips crystallized ginger

In a saucepan, bring the water to a boil over high heat. Add the sugar and stir until dissolved. Add the ginger slices, cover, and remove from the heat. Let stand for 5 minutes. For a stronger ginger flavor, let stand for 5–10 minutes longer. Strain the ginger infusion through a fine-mesh sieve into a glass jar, cover, and refrigerate until well chilled.

In a large pitcher, combine the lemon juice and ginger simple syrup. Stir in the sparkling water. Adjust to taste with more lemon juice or sparkling water.

Fill glasses with ice cubes and pour in the lemonade. Garnish each glass with a lemon slice and a crystallized ginger strip, then serve.

Blackberry Bellini

Pear Bellini

Strawberry Bellini   Peach Bellini

BELLINI BAR

MAKES 6 SERVINGS

Fruit puree of choice

1 bottle (750 ml) dry sparkling wine,
Champagne, or prosecco, chilled

Fresh fruit for garnish

BLACKBERRY PUREE

3 cups (375 g) blackberries

⅓ cup (70 g) superfine sugar,
or to taste

PEAR PUREE

4 pears, peeled, halved, cored,
and coarsely chopped

¼ cup (50 g) superfine sugar,
or to taste

1 tbsp pear brandy

STRAWBERRY PUREE

2½ cups (355 g) halved strawberries

¼ cup (50 g) superfine sugar,
or to taste

PEACH PUREE

4 ripe white or yellow peaches,
peeled, halved, pitted, and
coarsely chopped

¼ cup (50 g) superfine sugar,
or to taste

1 tsp fresh lemon juice

Traditionally a sparkling cocktail made with white peach puree and Italian prosecco, bellinis can be prepared with just about any type of sweetened fruit, and your favorite sparkling wine. Be sure to set a few bottles of sparkling wine on ice until well chilled, then put out a selection of fruit purees and some elegant glasses. Each fruit blend makes about 1 cup (250 ml) puree, or enough for one bottle's worth of sparkling wine.

Make 1 fruit puree at a time: In a blender, combine the fruit and sugar and, if using, the brandy or lemon juice. Blend to a smooth puree. Taste and add more sugar if needed; the puree should be sweet but not overly sweet. Pour the puree into a small pitcher or carafe, straining it through a coarse sieve if a smooth consistency is desired.

Fill Champagne flutes or wineglasses about one-third full with the fruit puree. Slowly fill the flutes or wineglasses with the sparkling wine. Stir briefly, garnish with fresh fruit, and serve.

BLOOD ORANGE MIMOSA

MAKES 4 SERVINGS

¼ cup (60 ml) orange liqueur

½ cup (120 ml) fresh blood orange juice

2 cups (475 ml) Champagne or sparkling white wine

1 slice blood orange, quartered

Pour 1 tbsp of the orange liqueur, 2 tbsp of the blood orange juice, and ½ cup (120 ml) of the Champagne into each chilled Champagne flute or wineglass. Stir briefly to mix. Garnish each flute with an orange quarter, then serve.

SUMMER FRUIT ROSÉ SANGRIA

MAKES 6–8 SERVINGS

1 bottle (750 ml) Provençal rosé

1¼ cups (300 ml) white cranberry juice

8 oz (225 g) raspberries

8 oz (225 g) blackberries or pitted cherries

1 nectarine, halved, pitted, and thinly sliced

1 white peach, halved, pitted, and thinly sliced

Ice cubes

In a large pitcher, combine the rosé, cranberry juice, raspberries, blackberries, nectarine, and peach. Stir well. Refrigerate until chilled and the flavors are blended, about 2 hours.

Fill glasses with ice cubes, pour in the sangria, and serve.

BALSAMIC BLOODY MARY

MAKES 4 SERVINGS

Ice cubes

1 cup (240 ml) vodka

2 cups (475 ml) tomato juice

1½ tbsp balsamic vinegar

1 tbsp prepared horseradish

1 tsp Worcestershire sauce

4 dashes of Tabasco sauce

¼ tsp celery salt

Juice of 2 limes

Freshly ground pepper

4 cherry tomatoes

4 green chiles

Fill tall glasses with ice cubes. In a large pitcher, combine the vodka, tomato juice, vinegar, horseradish, Worcestershire sauce, Tabasco sauce, celery salt, and lime juice. Stir well to combine and season to taste with pepper.

Pour into the glasses and garnish each glass with a cherry tomato and a chile speared on a cocktail pick. Serve at once.

MICHELADA

MAKES 4 SERVINGS

1 tbsp plus 1 tsp coarse sea salt

2 tsp chile powder

6 limes

Ice cubes

4 tsp Worcestershire sauce

Hot pepper sauce to taste

4 bottles (350 ml each) cold Mexican beer, such as Dos Equis or Pacifico

Have ready tall glasses or tumblers. Spread the salt and chile powder on a small, flat plate. Cut 2 of the limes into 4 wedges each. Run 1 lime wedge around the rim of each glass to moisten it and then dip the rim into the chile salt to coat it evenly. Reserve the remaining 4 lime wedges for garnish.

Juice the remaining 4 limes; you should have about ½ cup (120 ml) of lime juice. Fill each glass with several ice cubes. Add 2 tbsp of the lime juice, 1 tsp of the Worcestershire sauce, and a dash or so of hot pepper sauce to each glass. Pour 1 beer into each glass and stir gently. Garnish with a lime wedge and serve.

COLD BREW VANILLA
BEAN ICED COFFEE

MAKES 4 SERVINGS

1 cup (210 g) ground coffee

4 cups (950 ml) water

4 vanilla beans, split lengthwise (pods reserved for garnish)

1 cup (240 ml) milk of choice

¼ cup (50 g) sugar

Ice cubes

In a pitcher, stir the ground coffee into the water. Cover and let stand at room temperature for at least 12 hours.

In a saucepan, combine the vanilla beans, milk, and sugar. Bring the mixture to a simmer over medium heat and immediately remove from the heat. Allow to steep for about 20 minutes.

Strain the coffee through a fine-mesh sieve into a large bowl. Strain again through a coffee filter into a large, clean pitcher. Fill tumblers with ice cubes. Pour the coffee into the glasses, filling them to within 1 inch (2.5 cm) of the rim. Top each glass with ¼ cup (60 ml) of the vanilla-flavored milk. Garnish each drink with a vanilla bean pod and serve at once.

CHAI LATTE

MAKES 2 SERVINGS

1½-inch (4-cm) cinnamon stick

4 green cardamom pods

4 black cardamom pods

10 whole cloves

2 peppercorns

5 thin slices fresh ginger

1½ cups (350 ml) water

⅔ cup (160 ml) milk of choice

2 tbsp sugar

4 tsp Darjeeling tea leaves

In a saucepan, combine the cinnamon, cardamom pods, cloves, peppercorns, ginger slices, and water. Bring to a boil over medium heat, cover, reduce the heat to low, and simmer until the liquid is aromatic, about 10 minutes.

Add the milk and sugar and bring to a simmer over medium heat. Stir in the tea leaves, remove from the heat, cover, and let steep until the chai is the desired strength, 3–5 minutes.

If you have an espresso machine, steam and froth half of the chai according to the manufacturer's instructions. Return the chai to the pan. Pour the chai through a tea strainer or fine-mesh sieve into 2 mugs and top with the foam. Alternatively, reheat the chai over medium heat and pour into the mugs. Serve at once.

SPICY HOT COCOA

MAKES 4 SERVINGS

2 dried red chiles
6 tbsp (30 g) unsweetened cocoa powder
2 tbsp sugar
⅓ cup (80 ml) water
1½-inch (4-cm) cinnamon stick,
plus more for garnish
2½ cups (600 ml) milk of choice
Whipped cream for garnish (optional)

Open the chiles over a saucepan and release the seeds. Add the chile pods, cocoa powder, sugar, and water. Place over low heat and cook, stirring, until the mixture forms a smooth paste, 3–5 minutes.

Add the cinnamon stick and milk and stir until the paste is completely dissolved. Cook, stirring occasionally, until hot, about 5 minutes. Do not allow the milk to boil. Strain the hot cocoa into 4 mugs and garnish each with a cinnamon stick or a dollop of the whipped cream (if using). Serve at once.

SIDES

Homemade Chicken-Apple Sausage 147

Brown Sugar & Cardamom–Glazed Bacon 148

Cider-Glazed Pork Sausage 151

Spicy Black Beans with Chorizo 152

Roasted Rosemary Potatoes 152

Shredded Hash Browns 153

Roasted Vegetable Hash 155

HOMEMADE CHICKEN-APPLE SAUSAGE

MAKES 6-8 SERVINGS

1½ lb (680 g) boneless, skinless chicken breasts, frozen for 1 hour

¼ lb (115 g) sliced bacon, frozen for 1 hour

1 tbsp unsalted butter

2 Granny Smith apples, peeled, cored, grated, and squeezed dry

2 tsp coriander seeds

1 tsp fennel seeds

2 tsp white or black peppercorns

½ tsp kosher salt

½ tsp freshly grated nutmeg

¼ tsp cayenne pepper

2 tbsp olive oil

Making your own sausages at home means you can adjust the seasonings and flavors to taste. These are shaped into patties for easy prep, but if you have a sausage stuffer if you have a sausage stuffer, chill the meat mixture, then stuff it into hog casings and tie them into any size links you like.

Working in batches, place the chicken in a food processor and pulse until coarsely ground, 6–8 times. Transfer to a large bowl. Place the bacon in the processor and pulse until coarsely ground, 3–4 times. Add the bacon and butter to the chicken and stir until well blended. Add the apples to the bowl.

In a spice mill or in a mortar with a pestle, grind the coriander seeds, fennel seeds, and peppercorns to a medium-fine grind. Add the spices to the chicken mixture along with the salt, nutmeg, and cayenne. Mix with your fingertips until well blended.

Using your hands, shape the sausage mixture into 12–14 patties, each about 3 inches (7.5 cm) in diameter and ½ inch (12 mm) thick. (The patties can be made up to 1 day ahead; cover tightly and refrigerate.)

In a large frying pan, warm the oil over medium-high heat. Working in batches, add the patties and cook until golden brown, 3–4 minutes. Turn and cook until the patties are golden brown on the second sides, 3–4 minutes. Transfer to paper towels to drain briefly, then serve.

BROWN SUGAR & CARDAMOM–GLAZED BACON

MAKES 4–6 SERVINGS

1 lb (450 g) thick-cut lean bacon

⅓ cup (80 g) firmly packed light brown sugar

¼ tsp ground cardamom

¼ tsp freshly ground pepper

Salty bacon has a natural affinity for sweetness, whether glazed with honey, maple syrup, or brown sugar, as it is here. We added a pinch of cardamom and pepper to make it extra special, but you can leave out those spices if you like.

Preheat the oven to 350°F (180°C). Line the bottom and sides of a rimmed baking sheet with aluminum foil.

Arrange the bacon slices in a single layer on the prepared baking sheet. In a small bowl, toss together the brown sugar, cardamom, and pepper. Sprinkle the mixture over the bacon slices.

Bake the bacon, without turning the slices, for 25 minutes. Rotate the pan 180 degrees. Continue to bake the bacon, without turning, until dark brown but not quite crisp, 10–15 minutes longer. Using tongs, lift the bacon slices from the pan, gently shaking off the excess drippings, and transfer to paper towels to drain briefly.

Arrange the bacon on a warmed platter and serve at once.

CIDER-GLAZED PORK SAUSAGE

MAKES 4–6 SERVINGS

½ cup (120 ml) apple cider

2 tbsp light honey

2 tsp unsalted butter

1½ lb (680 g) fresh pork sausage links

Here, pan-seared pork sausage links are oven-glazed with a mixture of apple cider and honey, which caramelizes the exterior and adds tangy sweetness to the sausages. They make a wonderful side dish for breakfast or brunch during fall and winter.

Preheat the oven to 350°F (180°C). In a small bowl, stir together the cider and honey. Set aside.

In a large ovenproof frying pan, melt the butter over medium-high heat. When the butter foams, add the sausages and cook, turning occasionally, until browned, 7–8 minutes.

Brush the sausages with about one-third of the cider-honey mixture and and transfer the pan to the oven. Bake, turning once halfway through, until the juices run nearly clear when a sausage is pierced with a fork, about 10 minutes. Brush the sausages with half of the remaining cider-honey mixture and continue to bake until a glaze forms, about 2 minutes. Brush with the remaining cider-honey mixture and bake for 2 minutes longer.

Transfer the sausages to a warmed platter and serve at once.

SPICY BLACK BEANS WITH CHORIZO

MAKES 4–6 SERVINGS

1 tbsp olive oil

4 oz (115 g) fresh Mexican-style chorizo sausage, casings removed

1 yellow onion, chopped

1 red bell pepper, seeded and diced

1 jalapeño chile, seeded and minced

1 clove garlic, minced

2 cans (425 g each) black beans, drained and rinsed

½ cup (120 ml) low-sodium chicken broth

3 tbsp chopped fresh cilantro or oregano

Sour cream for serving (optional)

Mexican-style chorizo lends a deep flavor to these hearty beans, which are perfect alongside Tex-Mex Migas (page 22); Potato, Egg & Cheese Breakfast Tacos (page 17); or Huevos Rancheros (page 20). They are also great served on their own, topped with a fried egg and a side of warm tortillas.

In a medium saucepan, warm the oil over medium-high heat. Add the chorizo and cook, breaking it up with the side of a wooden spoon, until it begins to brown, about 8 minutes.

Add the onion, bell pepper, jalapeño, and garlic and reduce the heat to medium. Cook, stirring frequently, until the vegetables are tender, about 5 minutes. Add the beans and broth and bring to a simmer. Reduce the heat to medium-low and simmer until the liquid is reduced by half, about 15 minutes.

Using the side of the wooden spoon, crush some of the beans in the saucepan to thicken the juices. Stir in 2 tbsp of cilantro. Spoon onto plates or into bowls and garnish with the remaining 1 tbsp of cilantro and a dollop of sour cream (if using). Serve at once.

ROASTED ROSEMARY POTATOES

MAKES 4–6 SERVINGS

1½ lb (680 g) small red potatoes, each about 1 inch (2.5 cm) in diameter

2 tbsp olive oil

Kosher salt and freshly ground pepper

2 tbsp minced fresh rosemary

Roasted potatoes are a simple, hands-off dish that can accompany nearly any egg dish in this book. Use red potatoes, or try cubed Yukon gold or even fingerling potatoes. The rosemary adds a terrific fragrance to the finished dish.

Preheat the oven to 350°F (180°C).

Place the potatoes in a shallow baking dish just large enough to hold them snugly in a single layer. Drizzle with the oil and turn to coat well. Season generously with salt and pepper. Sprinkle with the rosemary and turn again to coat.

Roast the potatoes, turning once or twice, until the skins wrinkle and the potatoes can be easily pierced with a fork, about 1¼ hours.

Transfer the potatoes to a bowl and serve hot or at room temperature.

SHREDDED HASH BROWNS

MAKES 4–6 SERVINGS

1 tbsp unsalted butter

1 small yellow onion, finely chopped

1 small red bell pepper, seeded and finely chopped

1½ tsp kosher salt, plus more as needed

¼ tsp freshly ground pepper, plus more as needed

3 large russet potatoes, about 1½ lb (680 g) total, peeled

4 tbsp (60 ml) avocado oil or canola oil

Crisp on the outside and tender on the inside, hash browns are a mainstay of any classic breakfast restaurant. To make sure your homemade ones are just as good, be sure to soak the grated potatoes in water to release their starch and squeeze them as dry as possible. Pan-fry the potatoes undisturbed to develop a crisp crust on the bottom, then carefully flip them to brown the second side.

In a heavy frying pan, preferably cast iron, melt the butter over medium heat. Add the onion and bell pepper and cook, stirring occasionally, until tender, about 8 minutes. Season to taste with salt and pepper. Transfer to a medium bowl.

Shred the potatoes. Line a colander with cheesecloth and set the colander in the sink or over a large bowl. Transfer the potatoes to the colander and twist the cheesecloth tightly into a pouch, squeezing out the moisture. Let the potatoes drain for 15 minutes. Squeeze the cheesecloth again, then transfer the potatoes to another large bowl. Add the 1½ tsp salt and ¼ tsp pepper and stir well.

In the same frying pan, warm 2 tbsp of the oil over medium-high heat. Add the potato mixture and spread into a thick cake. Reduce the heat to medium, cover, and cook until golden brown and crisp underneath, about 6 minutes. Using a wide metal spatula, slide the potato cake onto a plate. Warm the remaining 2 tbsp oil in the pan. Carefully flip the potato cake, browned side up, into the pan. Cook until golden brown and crisp on the second side, about 6 minutes.

Slide the potatoes onto a platter. Return the onion mixture to the pan and cook, stirring often, until heated through, about 1 minute. Heap the onion mixture onto the potatoes and serve.

ROASTED VEGETABLE HASH

MAKES 6–8 SERVINGS

1½ lb (680 g) orange-fleshed sweet potatoes, peeled and cut into small cubes

1½ lb (680 g) Yukon gold potatoes, peeled and cut into small cubes

2 tbsp olive oil

1 yellow onion, chopped

1 red bell pepper, seeded and chopped

1 jalapeño chile, seeded and minced

1 cup (170 g) fresh or thawed frozen corn kernels

1½ tsp ground cumin

3 tbsp chopped fresh cilantro, plus more for garnish

Kosher salt and freshly ground pepper

Plain yogurt for serving

Lime wedges for serving

A mixture of orange sweet potatoes, Yukon gold potatoes, onion, peppers, and sweet corn kernels, this vegetarian hash makes a terrific side dish or can stand on its own as a main, especially if topped with poached eggs. Don't forgo the dollop of plain yogurt and squeeze of lime as this really makes the hash shine.

Preheat the oven to 400°F (200°C). Lightly oil a large rimmed baking sheet.

Place all the potatoes on the prepared baking sheet. Drizzle with 1 tbsp of the oil, toss to coat the potatoes, and spread in an even layer. Roast for 30 minutes. Turn the potatoes and continue roasting until lightly browned and tender, about 15 minutes. Keep warm.

Meanwhile, in a large frying pan, heat the remaining 1 tbsp oil over medium heat. Add the onion, bell pepper, and jalapeño and cook, stirring occasionally, until the vegetables are tender, about 10 minutes. Stir in the corn and cook until heated through, about 3 minutes. Stir in the cumin and cook until fragrant, about 30 seconds. Add the potatoes and cilantro and stir to combine. Season with salt and pepper.

Spoon the hash into bowls. Top each serving with a dollop of yogurt and a sprinkle of additional cilantro. Serve with lime wedges.

BASICS

Pico de Gallo

MAKES ABOUT 2½ CUPS (625 G)

2 large ripe tomatoes, seeded and diced
½ cup (75 g) finely chopped yellow onion
3 tbsp minced fresh cilantro
1 tbsp fresh lime juice
½ jalapeño chile, seeded and minced, or more to taste
Kosher salt

In a nonreactive bowl, stir together the tomatoes, onion, cilantro, lime juice, and jalapeño. Season with salt. Cover and let stand at room temperature for at least 30 minutes or up to 3 hours.

Dijon Vinaigrette

MAKES ABOUT ½ CUP (120 ML)

¼ cup (60 ml) olive oil
3 tbsp rice vinegar
1 tbsp Dijon mustard
1 tsp honey or agave nectar, to taste
Kosher salt

In a jar, combine the oil, vinegar, mustard, honey, and salt and shake until well blended.

Hollandaise Sauce

MAKES ABOUT 1½ CUPS (375 ML)

4 large egg yolks
2 tbsp fresh lemon juice
Kosher salt and freshly ground pepper
1 cup (250 g) unsalted butter

In a blender, combine the egg yolks, lemon juice, ⅛ tsp salt, and a few grinds of pepper. In a small saucepan, melt the butter over medium heat. With the blender running, slowly add the warm melted butter through the vent in the lid, processing until the sauce is thick and smooth. Taste and adjust the seasoning with salt and pepper. If the sauce is too thick, add a little water to thin it.

Transfer the hollandaise sauce to a heatproof bowl. Cover and place over but not touching hot, not simmering, water in a saucepan to keep warm. (For a less lemony sauce, use 1 tbsp fresh lemon juice and add 1 tbsp water.)

Lemon Curd

MAKES 1¼ CUPS (310 ML)

2 large eggs
2 large egg yolks
1 tsp finely grated lemon zest
⅓ cup (80 ml) fresh lemon juice, strained
1 cup (250 g) sugar
6 tbsp (90 g) unsalted butter, cut into pieces

In the top of a double boiler, combine the eggs, egg yolks, lemon juice, sugar, and butter. Place over but not touching gently simmering water and whisk steadily until the sugar dissolves and the butter melts. Continue to whisk until the curd coats the back of a spoon, about 8 minutes. Do not let the curd boil.

Strain the curd through a medium-mesh sieve into a bowl. Stir in the lemon zest. Cover with plastic wrap, pressing it gently onto the surface of the curd to prevent a skin from forming. Poke a few holes in the plastic with the tip of a knife to let steam escape. Let cool, then refrigerate until well chilled, about 3 hours, or for up to 3 days.

Single-Crust Pie Dough

MAKES ENOUGH FOR ONE 9-INCH (23-CM) PIE OR TART

1¼ cups (155 g) all-purpose flour
¼ tsp kosher salt
6 tbsp (90 g) very cold unsalted butter, cut into cubes
6 tbsp (90 ml) ice water, plus more if needed

In the bowl of a food processor, stir together the flour and salt. Sprinkle the butter over the top and pulse for a few seconds, until the butter is just slightly broken up into the flour but is still in visible pieces. Evenly sprinkle the water over the flour mixture, then process until the mixture just starts to come together. Dump the dough into a large lock-top plastic bag and press into a flat disk. Refrigerate the dough for 30 minutes or up to 1 day, or freeze for up to 1 month.

Toasting Nuts and Coconut

Preheat the oven to 325°F (165°C). Spread the nuts or coconut out on a rimmed baking sheet and bake, stirring often, until fragrant and lightly toasted, 5–10 minutes, depending on the nuts or coconut.

INDEX

BREAKFAST & BRUNCH: 100+ RECIPES TO START THE DAY

Conceived and produced by Weldon Owen International
in collaboration with Williams Sonoma, Inc.
3250 Van Ness Avenue, San Francisco, CA 94109

A Weldon Owen Production
PO Box 3088
San Rafael, CA 94912
www.weldonowen.com

ISBN: 979-8-88674-121-6

Manufactured in China by Insight Editions
10 9 8 7 6 5 4 3 2 1

weldon**owen**

CEO Raoul Goff
Publisher Roger Shaw
Associate Publisher Amy Marr
Publishing Director Katie Killebrew
Assistant Editor Kayla Belser
VP Creative Chrissy Kwasnik
Design Manager Megan Sinead Bingham
Production Designer Jean Hwang
VP Manufacturing Alix Nicholaeff
Sr Production Manager Joshua Smith
Sr Production Manager, Subsidiary Rights
Lina s Palma-Temena

Photographer & Prop Stylist Erin Scott
Food Stylist Lillian Kang

Weldon Owen wishes to thank the following people for their generous support in producing
this book: Kris Balloun, Kim Laidlaw, Rachel Markowitz, Elizabeth Parson, and Sharon Silva.

Insight Editions, in association with Roots of Peace, will plant two trees for each tree used in
the manufacturing of this book. Roots of Peace is an internationally renowned humanitarian
organization dedicated to eradicating land mines worldwide and converting war-torn lands into
productive farms and wildlife habitats. Roots of Peace will plant two million fruit and nut trees
in Afghanistan and provide farmers there with the skills and support necessary for sustainable
land use.